Well-Rounded

Well-Rounded

Mind Health Fitness

BY ALEXANDER PIERCE

WWW.WELL-ROUNDED.ORG

The publisher and the author do not make any guarantee or other promise as to any results that may be obtained from using the contents of this book. You should never make any investment decision without first consulting with your own financial advisor and conducting your own research and due diligence. Although the author and publisher have made every effort to ensure that the information in this book was correct at press time, the author and publisher do not assume and hereby disclaim any liability to any party for any loss, damage, or disruption caused by errors or omissions, whether such errors or omissions result from negligence, accident, or any other cause. This book is not intended as a substitute for the medical advice of physicians. The content of this book is for informational purposes only and is not intended to diagnose, treat, cure, or prevent any condition or disease. Please con-sult with your own physician or healthcare specialist regarding any suggestions and recommendations made in this book. You should understand that when participating in any exercise or exercise program, there is the possibility of physical injury and side effects. If you engage in any exercise, exercise technique, or exercise program, you agree that you do so at your own risk, are voluntarily participating in these activities, assume all risk of injury to yourself, and agree to release and discharge the publisher and the author from any and all claims or causes of action, known or unknown, arising out of the contents of this book. The use of this book implies your acceptance of this disclaimer.

Copyright © 2022 by Alexander D. Pierce
All rights reserved.
Published by Well-Rounded, LLC Hillsboro, OR

First Edition: September 2022
ISBN: 979-8-9869077-0-3 (Paperback)
ISBN: 979-8-9869077-1-0 (eBook)
ISBN: 979-8-9869077-2-7 (Hardcover)
Library of Congress Control Number: 2022917175

Learn more: www.well-rounded.org
Contact: contact@well-rounded.org

ACKNOWLEDGEMENTS

I am extremely grateful to all who have stood by me during the writing of this book. Most notably my son, for his encouragement and understanding.

I am thankful for all my experiences and connections with people that have helped me to understand things from different perspectives.

A special thanks to my professors for their teachings and valuable feedback.

Finally, I wish to express gratitude for all my experience with patients and clients as they have helped me to understand the great challenges people have, and that it is the individual person who has the most control over their health and happiness.

CONTENTS

INTRODUCTION	1
PART I: Mind	**5**
CHAPTER 1: Brain & Mind	7
CHAPTER 2: Understanding Stress	29
CHAPTER 3: Establishing & Maintaining Relationships	49
CHAPTER 4: Financial Understanding	77
CHAPTER 5: Ethics	93
PART II: Health	**127**
CHAPTER 6: Understanding Health	129
CHAPTER 7: Understanding Nutrition	149
PART III: Fitness	**171**
CHAPTER 8: Motivation & Obstacles	173
CHAPTER 9: Warmups & Stretching	187
CHAPTER 10: Balance & Core	195
CHAPTER 11: Strength & Power	205
CHAPTER 12: Endurance & Alternatives	217
LIVE WELL	227
ABOUT THE AUTHOR	229

INTRODUCTION

What comes to mind when you think of the word "well-rounded"? You may imagine a well-educated person who has achieved substantial teaching and knowledge. They may have great ambition and many achievements. They may appear confident, healthy, and energetic and treat people with regard and show compassion for them. They may have many close relationships with people, who admire this person and say great things about their character.

Well-rounded is a fine term to use when complimenting a person such as this; someone who seems as though they are well-experienced in life. It's likely they reached this point through great struggles, as we all do—those that appear well-rounded may have endured great challenges and failures in order to now captivate others.

Despite these challenges, they have developed their mind and body to the extent that others have noticed and so respect them. If you were to ask someone such as this if they believe they are well-rounded, they will likely say they are not. If you believe that you are well-rounded, then you may feel you have nothing left to learn. Well-rounded is an appropriate compliment to give to people who you recognize for their achievements, their endearing personalities, and how well they treat others. However, there will always be more ways in which you can develop yourself.

A person may then ask, why would I want to strive for something I know cannot be entirely achieved? The answer to this question is that in aiming to be well-rounded, you work on all areas of being human and maximize all aspects of your potential. You may never be able to consider yourself well-rounded, but in pursuit of it, you will accomplish much more.

You will attain great understanding as well as improved communication, enabling you to have many great relationships with people who will come to respect you. You will excel in your career and become financially stable enough to pursue your interests. You will achieve great levels of health and fitness so that you feel good and enjoy life more. You can then pass on your quality knowledge to others, which they can use to develop themselves. These are all aspects that will improve during your pursuit to become well-rounded and which will allow you to live well. Through this endeavor to be your best self, perhaps someone might one day believe you to be well-rounded.

This book conveys many useful strategies to improve yourself so that you can overcome barriers and enjoy life. These concepts are presented in an uncomplicated, remarkably simple way to provide quality information you can understand and find use for. There are great methods for organization and efficiency so that you can maximize your time, as well as ways to gain more control over your finances, stress, health, and fitness. This allows you to improve both how you feel and how effective you can be.

You can combine this information with your experiences and knowledge to further develop yourself, design new ways to connect with

Introduction

others, and pursue your interests.

May this book inspire you to develop your mind and body in great ways.

May you live well.

PART I

Mind

If you strive to develop yourself often, it may allow you to live your greatest life possible. The first section of this book talks about the mind and stress; it considers certain stressors that affect your mind's capacity for health and improvement. You begin here, as your mind is the first and foremost part of your health that allows you to manage stress and improve all other aspects of your body. Additionally, if you have a healthy mind, you can manage your responsibilities and pursuits more effectively.

Examining how the brain and mind work will improve your understanding of its adaptability, letting you consider not only how you can maintain your mind for it to function well, but how you can also enhance it. Learning about the manifestation of *stress* within you and its effects on your mind and body will help you to better understand and recognize when it occurs.

It's also important to identify stressors and where they come from. Things such as poor relationships with people, self-criticism, and financial troubles can all be triggers for stress. If you increase your awareness of these stressors and develop skills to manage them, you can reduce their burden on you.

It may be interesting to learn that your ethics can also affect the health of your mind. Developing a greater sense of right and wrong will let you make choices that prevent confusion and remorse. You can also achieve happiness through helping others, and you can avoid consequences that result from immoral decisions. Addressing the health and performance of your mind will better equip you to handle problems when they arise and allow a greater ability to achieve your aspirations, whatever they may be.

CHAPTER 1

Brain & Mind

The brain is an incredibly complex organ. We have studied it extensively and yet there is still so much we don't understand about it. It consists of a network of neurons within various structures that have automatic functions like controlling your breathing and heartbeat, as well as allowing you perception, emotions, and the thoughts that incorporate who you are.

These cognitive abilities result in vastly differing minds capable of understanding, reasoning, and reacting to a given environment—each with an individual personality. They are also constantly changing; you are different now than you were a moment before. This continues throughout your life every time you experience something. The more you use your mind, the more connections you make, and the further you improve your understanding of things.

If you wish to have a healthy functioning brain and a well-developed mind, you should manage stress, focus on good nutrition, and challenge yourself frequently. This chapter describes certain structures and functions of the central nervous system, and how you can reduce harm, slow decline, and improve mental performance.

Actively improving your mind requires a commitment of time and energy, especially considering that the greatest benefits come from encouraging yourself to learn challenging things.

Why should you make this kind of effort?

Well, most of your brain development happens when you're young. Once you reach adulthood, your brain will decline as you age, resulting in decreased capacity for learning, reacting, and remembering. Mental exercises can slow this cognitive decline, which is reason enough to stimulate your mind daily. As well as this, there are many other benefits, such as improving your knowledge to enable greater understanding and decision making, and bettering your communication skills, which may lead to new opportunities, improved work performance, and stronger relationships. Additionally, the increased confidence you gain will allow you to enjoy life more, and when complications *do* present themselves, you will be able to handle them more effectively.

Anatomy and Functions of the Nervous System

It's helpful to have at least a general understanding of your brain's anatomy and how it functions. Our central nervous system is made up of both the brain and spinal cord. You have motor nerves that carry signals from the brain to the spinal cord and then out to different parts the body. It is these signals that allow you to do things such as walk around or pick things up. You also have sensory nerves that transmit signals back to the brain, allowing you to sense things in your immediate environment such as the temperature of water or the feeling of a cat's fur. The brain perceives these sensations as the body experiences them and may combine them with input from your other senses, such as what you see or hear. It then will interpret the information and store anything perceived as relevant as a memory in a part of the brain called the hippocampus.

The brain itself is a very complex organ with an arrangement of neurons in various structures that work very quickly to perform tasks —many are autonomic processes, such as breathing, digesting, and controlling body temperature. You also have an awareness of self and an ability to perceive and reflect on emotions, thoughts, and things externally. Our minds are unique, both due to genetics, and, as previously mentioned, because they change each time you experience something. The brain can also attach emotions to memories, which will be discussed in a later chapter. Memories can later be retrieved to associate with new experiences, which further expands your knowledge.

There are three major parts of the brain. These have different roles but work collectively. The cerebrum is the largest part of your brain and has a left and right hemisphere. The two hemispheres communicate with each other via the corpus callosum, a structure of nerve fibers located between the two sections. Our left hemisphere is mostly responsible for your creativity, such as your artistic and musical abilities. The right side is more often responsible for speech, writing, reasoning, and arithmetic. The cerebrum of the brain is larger and more developed in humans than in other animals; it's what makes us so advanced and allows you to learn and communicate more so than most other species in the world.

The next major part of the brain is the cerebellum. This section is located bellow the cerebrum and is responsible for coordinating posture, balance, and muscle movement. This structure is essential to how smoothly you can position and move your body. The third major structure is the brainstem, this connects the brain to the spinal cord. The brainstem is responsible for our unconscious functions.

Within the brain, your mind is constantly changing and making new connections each time you experience something; whether you're reading a book, having a conversation, or walking in the park. This ability to constantly adapt and change is called "neuroplasticity." It allows you the ability to improve your mind using anything you perceive in your external environment, or from your internal thoughts. You should challenge your mind frequently to improve its capacity for knowledge and decision making, but before this it's important to discuss how you can keep your brain and mind healthy.

Taking care of the brain means ensuring proper nutrition and protecting it from physical and emotional trauma. Nutrition is important because what you consume each day will either support healthy brain function or harm it—which can decrease your ability to learn and form new memories. Adding beneficial foods to your diet will meet your brain's needs for the structural maintenance of neurons, neurogenesis (the creation of new neurons), and synaptic transmissions (how the nerves communicate). Conversely, foods that cause the poor functioning of cells should be reduced or eliminated where possible to avoid inflammation in both the brain and body. Poor nutrition can slow down the firing of neurons in the brain, causing physical symptoms such as brain fog, slow thinking, and problems with memory.

Macronutrients

The brain requires adequate amounts of macro and micronutrients for healthy functioning. Macronutrients include healthy fats, proteins, and carbohydrates. These nutrients are important for brain cells to produce energy and develop their structures. The brain is primarily made of fat, most of which is omega-3 fatty acids. These cannot be made by the body so you must consume them from healthy sources such as fish, flaxseeds, and nuts. Your doctor can also recommend omega-3 supplements, which can bridge gaps in your diet if the supplement is properly manufactured. Saturated fats are not ideal as they can be inflammatory to cells in the brain and cause problems throughout the body. These should be replaced with healthy fats, such as extra-virgin olive oil, when cooking or adding to foods.

Protein is the second largest matter in the brain and is required by every cell in the body. Proteins have many roles and are essential for the proper communication of brain cells—therefore, deficiencies can lead to a decrease in cognitive functions. Healthy sources of protein such as fish low in toxins and nuts (such as walnuts and pecans) will also aid brain functions.

Carbohydrates are the brain's preferred fuel source as these are the simplest way for the brain to get energy. Carbohydrates from whole foods are healthier as the brain will get a slow, steady, and long-term source of energy from them as they are slow releasing. Simple carbohydrates are only a brief source of energy and can be quite harmful to brain cells as well as increase the body's risk of insulin resistance. It can also result in inflammation and damage to brain cells.

Large amounts, and long-term consumption, of simple sugars can lead to cognitive decline as well as many other negative health effects. Limiting refined sugars as much as possible will provide you many health benefits including a healthier, better functioning brain.

Micronutrients

Proper levels of micronutrients such as vitamins and minerals are necessary for things such as supporting brain cell functions and the neural activity between them—for example, allowing the proper function and synthesis of neurotransmitters (the chemicals needed for nerves to communicate with each other). These nutrients can mostly be achieved through a healthy diet, however many people are still deficient in them. This can be caused by things such as inadequate intake from your diet and poor absorption. An annual visit to your doctor can help you check for these levels in your blood to determine whether you are deficient. If you feel low in energy or just don't feel right, then it may be worth it to check your blood for proper levels of these nutrients.

Having optimal health helps you to feel better and enable a greater performance from both your mind and body. If you're struggling to attain a proper diet, there are many registered dietitians that can assist in creating proper food lists and can recommend supplements to help you accurately correct your nutrition.

Antioxidants

As an adult, your brain's ability for neurogenesis (the formation of new neurons) decreases, so it is important to protect the brain cells that you have to allow for as much growth as possible.

Polyphenols are an antioxidant found in plant-based foods and they can protect you from things such as free radicals and oxidants, many of which are toxic to you. Free radicals and oxidants are created in the body naturally during cellular metabolism but can also enter the body following exposure to pollution, smoking, or other chemicals. Antioxidants protect you by neutralizing these harmful toxins, protecting your brain against aging and disease.

One type of polyphenol you can incorporate into your diet is flavonoids. These healthy plant chemicals are found in deeply-colored fruits such as blueberries, in vegetables such as kale, and can also be found in cocoa, tea, and spices such as turmeric. If you can add these foods to your diet, you can reduce the levels of many harmful toxins in your body.

Consuming many anti-inflammatory foods such as leafy greens and berries multiple days each week (and decreasing consumption of inflammatory saturated fats and refined sugars) is a great way to sustain your brain for optimal functioning as well as slowing aging and decreasing the risk of health conditions and diseases.

Exposure to Toxins

There are various ways you can be exposed to toxins that will negatively impact your brain: Drugs, alcohol, smoking, and chemicals used at home or work can be very harmful to you. These are all substances that can cause damage to brain cells and interfere with brain signals, which can slow down and interrupt thinking. They also decrease your reaction speed and can cause the loss of both short- and long-term memory. Reducing, or entirely removing these sources of toxins can benefit you by improving both your energy levels, and the performance of your mind and body.

Sometimes, all it takes is replacing a dependance on drugs or alcohol with a healthy activity such as exercise, hobbies, or a new business endeavor. We can be surprisingly capable when we remove unhealthy and time-consuming activities from our lives.

It's important to assess your home and workplace for chemicals you use daily that may cause harm when you inhale them into the lungs or absorb them through the skin. Knowing the potential these chemicals have for harming you, you should use barrier precautions such as gloves, goggles, and masks—as well as ensuring good ventilation—if you wish to protect your brain cells.

Sleep

Another problem that many encounter is insufficient sleep—particularly a lack of deep sleep. During deep sleep, your brain sorts through your experiences and disregards anything unnecessary while utilizing more essential information to develop memories and create new ones.

This strengthens neurons and creates new connections, improving your knowledge and understanding. It also balances neurotransmitters, tiny chemicals that allow the nerves to communicate with each other; these are important for how you think and feel. The body and mind go through many stages of healing during sleep. Therefore, without it, you may experience delayed responses, problems concentrating, and difficulties learning and forming new memories.

Getting an appropriate amount of sleep will benefit you greatly, as it will maintain your brain's health and allow you to build stronger neural connections.

Physical Trauma

Sustaining physical trauma to the brain is a very quick way to damage it. Our brains are floating in a solution called cerebrospinal fluid, which allows it some shock absorption in light and moderate activities, but this does not prevent the brain from injury if the force is too great. You must always be assessing your environment for hazards that may result in head trauma. Falling, sports injuries, and motor vehicle accidents are top contributors to these kinds of incidents.

You don't need to limit yourself entirely from the things you like do and the places you go, but you should always take your brain into consideration. Taking safety measures allows you to continue the fun and important activities you enjoy doing and reduce your risks at the same time. Most brain trauma is preventable if precautions are taken; wearing seatbelts and helmets or clearing walkways of debris are just a few simple safeguards.

Emotional Trauma and Stress

Emotional stress and trauma can also damage both your brain and mind; these may lead to mental illness, health problems, and cause damage to brain cells and their ability to function. You may be at greater risk for emotional problems due to your genetics, or after difficult experiences such as poor relationships, shock, loss, abuse, and financial stress.

This book describes many stressors to look for in your life.

Stress, which is discussed in the next chapter, can promote inflammation, harm brain cells, and slow down, or block the progress of new connections in the brain. Emotional regulation is something that many struggle with each day, and it can make it difficult when you want to improve the performance of your mind.

Fortunately, many people have friends and family that have helped them previously and will continue to do so because they care for you. There are also many specialists, such as doctors and therapists, who can help you regulate your stress and health issues so you can improve your mind with less barriers in your way.

Our brains can be quite resilient; however, they can also become overworked from the persistent workings of your mind and stress. Many college students experience this if they have trouble spreading out their work evenly. They tend to cram in studying to catch up and overstress themselves. This can result in learning less and poor performance on assignments and tests.

Working adults encounter this when they have deadlines at work, difficult superiors and coworkers, numerous family responsibilities, or unrealistic expectations they put on themselves.

Children can get stressed when they are constantly critiqued and corrected by teachers, peers, and parents. There's a lot of pressure put on you all throughout life, and this can be harmful to your mind and body if not managed well.

Breaks and Meditation

You can reduce stress with short breaks and meditation. Taking a break when things get difficult will allow your brain to relax so it can organize all the information you are absorbing. Going for a walk, having a snack, or even doing something fun for short while will decrease stress and allow you to return to your work with a fresh mindset.

If you feel intensifying frustration, tension, and worry, it's a good time to take a break. Stepping away from a problem to take a moment and then coming back to it later can really make a difference. Additionally, you can sometimes detect this in others, and reminding them to take a break may help lessen their troubles, too.

You've likely heard that meditation is relaxing and reduces stress. This is true for both the mind and body. Meditation can help reduce overall stress so that you can go about your day stronger and more relaxed, which can help you to handle new stressors better. It can also be very helpful at the end of your day when you want to wind down, relax, and have a better quality of sleep.

Meditation has been shown to help balance the neurotransmitters in your brain so that you can feel and perform better. Taking time to close your eyes and clear your mind for an extended period will allow for healing and less tension.

More will be discussed about the benefits of meditation and how you can achieve such a state in the next chapter.

Exercise

With all the known health benefits you can achieve through exercise, it may come as no surprise to learn that it can considerably improve the health of your brain as well. During exercise, there is an increase in blood flow to the brain, which increases the amount of nutrients it receives. This is important as blood is the delivery system for oxygen, glucose, protein building amino acids, and micronutrients that brain cells require to build and maintain themselves.

Exercise is also very effective at helping the brain improve memory, thinking, and focus because it helps protect neurons and encourage the creation of new ones. Additionally, it can help you sleep better at night allowing you to consolidate your memories and the other benefits discussed previously.

Exercise also decreases stress and increases endorphins, which are hormones that make you feel better. This can greatly improve your mindset and how you feel. Providing you're not overdoing it and you get the proper nutrition, your body and mind will benefit greatly from exercising many days each week.

Mind

Just as complex as the brain, the mind is also exceptionally difficult to understand entirely. There are billions of neurons in the brain that send chemical signals to communicate with each other. Science has yet to determine how the mind is borne from this, but we know that some thoughts arise automatically, likely suggestive from the subconscious mind, and others are intentional, such as if you want to access your memories to answer a question.

Our subconscious works on autopilot, protecting you and sensing opportunities. It can communicate with the conscious mind, which determines how, and whether you should, proceed. You can also use your conscious mind to communicate with your subconscious to remember how to ride a bike or access memories purposefully.

However, there is still so much we don't understand about the mind and many more interesting answers still await discovery. Many of the risks explained for the brain, such as stress, abuse, poor sleep, and lack of exercise, can be very harmful to your mind as well. It is also susceptible to harm from frustration and self-criticism. This will be expanded on in later chapters, but it's important that you encourage yourself to improve, safeguard yourself from harm, and remain aware that mistakes will happen as they are part of learning.

Improving the Mind and Slowing Decline

The mind is an amazing phenomenon that we are each presented with, and our minds are all so exceptionally different from one another. This makes for the incredible and diverse world that we each see in different ways.

Because of neuroplasticity, the mind's ability to change through experience, we each develop our knowledge from our own experiences, which are unique to us.

Likewise, this is how you can improve your mind to a greater extent: By taking advantage of your mind's capacity for change. You can increase your mental speed and knowledge, allowing you greater understanding and decision making. And, when you do this, you also preserve better functioning of your mind for longer.

Not only can you slow the cognitive decline that occurs due to aging and lack of use, but you can also improve it. With frequent use, neurons can strengthen their connections with other neurons; they can also grow and make new ones. However, if unused, neurons and their connections can be lost.

You can improve your mind casually using everyday experiences, but there is much more you can do if you wish to intentionally improve and slow down this natural decline. Just as lifting weights enhances muscles and walking improves bones, exercising the brain will maintain and enhance your cognitive abilities.

Improving Through Learning

Learning can be complicated and uncomfortable at times, but it's how you improve, and you can benefit considerably from it. Learning is challenging because things are, at that moment you seek to learn them, unknown to you. If you wish to learn something new, you may need to learn many parts individually before you can understand the whole concept—and this takes time and mental effort.

You will also make mistakes that discourage you from learning. But that difficulty is what allows your mind to change and develop through making new connections, building more knowledge, and slowing loss. It's often difficult the first time you attempt to learn something new, but once you take a break and come back to it, you find it much easier to understand each time you return to it.

This is how learning works, through delivering information to your mind and then taking breaks to allow rest and the consolidation of memories to give you a fresh perspective and knowledge when you see it again.

As mentioned before, sleep allows you even greater consolidation of memories and you will understand something even more if you return to it the next day. It's incredibly rewarding when you do understand something that was previously challenging and difficult, especially when the stress and frustration fades away.

Difficulty is what allows you to improve, so you don't have to let it discourage you from learning. Exercise is difficult, yet it yields results when you perform it often. Going to work is difficult, but it provides an income for expenses and for you to save for things you like to do. There are many benefits to exercising your mind.

Challenging the Mind

Challenging your mind each day is exceptionally good for maintaining and improving its condition. New knowledge can also take the place of previous misinformation. Unfortunately, creating opportunities to learn can be very difficult if you have a busy life.

It's helpful to have a list of simple things you can do during your down time and set certain blocks of time aside for things that require more concentration. You can read a book in many places, but if you want to read and write a reflection, you may want to have a quiet setting for it.

This is also true of learning a language, taking classes, and many other things that require deep concentration without distractions. It benefits you to challenge yourself with things you want to improve and gain skill at, and this drive can make learning easier, fun, and practical.

On the other hand, you can easily play a game of chess on your phone or do a crossword puzzle to pass the time in a waiting room or on a lunch break no matter where you are.

Improving Through Interaction

Just having conversations with people can be a great way to develop your mind. This can be with people you know well, or anyone you happen to meet and begin speaking with. Conversations with people can help you improve your speech because you are actively practicing the skill, and memory because you are constantly accessing it to deliver information.

You can also learn new ideas from other people because they have many different experiences outside your own. Conversations require you to think on the spot and use your knowledge instantly as you don't always have many resources to support you in the moment. This can help you not only improve the response time of your thinking but may also help you realize that you may need a firmer understanding of things you thought to be true before explaining them to others.

Likewise, you can sometimes get great feedback from others if they are confident enough to point out your misconceptions. You can learn so much from finding people that are highly educated or have many experiences and enjoy sharing their knowledge with you.

During conversations, you also secrete hormones that make you feel good. So speaking with people will allow you to build emotional connections with others and feel better at the same time. Additionally, communication with others gives you opportunities to network and make connections with people that can result in new friendships, business contacts, and personal relationships. It's also symbiotic, because the people you talk to are also learning from you.

Improving Through Reading

Reading is one of the best ways to improve your knowledge, understanding, and speaking abilities. Both fiction and nonfiction books allow your mind to absorb new knowledge and insight from the writer's words and style.

Fiction books open you up to different possibilities and many things you have never imagined before. These can inspire you to use your own imagination and creativity. Reading fiction for enjoyment can also help you reduce stress and allow you to escape external pressures and cycling thoughts.

Additionally, you may sometimes find yourself analyzing the information you are reading for clues so that you can make predictions about the outcome of the story. Doing this can improve your critical thinking skills and practicing it often will allow you to incorporate these skills into your daily life. Making predictions and deducing future events is a great skill to have if used well.

Fictional books are a fantastic way for you to improve your knowledge, creativity, and critical thinking.

Nonfiction can be very valuable for you to improve your understanding and knowledge about real things in the world. It teaches you what others have concluded about organic and inorganic matter, space, and time. You can learn how things are invented, how they work, and their uses. You can learn about history from different perspectives and how we have evolved into different cultures and societies.

Having a greater awareness of many different things in the world and their various parts, functions, and philosophies will give your mind more to work with.

There are so many resources available to obtain knowledge that you really can learn just about anything. Public libraries have a variety of books that are free to read. The internet provides countless ways to learn through online textbooks, labelled images, and videos explaining difficult concepts. You can also access scientific articles and studies that support certain theories for evidence-based learning.

Learning about real things in the world can help you with your own projects, inventions, and ideas about how other things might work. Wouldn't it be nice to contribute something new to the world that came from your own mind?

There is so much that is yet to be discovered, and you are only limited by your drive to learn and apply your knowledge.

Improving Through Writing and Reflecting

You can further the knowledge you gain through reading by writing down a reflection afterwards. Writing your interpretation of what you read will help you to understand it better and remember it for longer. Writing reflections can also give you new ideas and improve your writing skills.

Additionally, it allows you to express your thoughts and explain what you believe about the material. Furthermore, you will likely learn more because you may need to examine the text or research it deeper to fully comprehend it before putting in writing.

As a result, you will also become more capable of explaining it to others. College students use this method to study for tests because if they can teach what they have learned to someone else, they should understand it well enough to answer questions about it. Just writing in general can also be great for the mind. Writing about your day, your feelings and things that trouble you, and describing the world around you are great ways for you to express and learn about yourself.

Writing requires your mind to do a great deal of work to explain what you understand and believe. In return, you improve your creativity, memory, communication, and critical thinking skills. Writing often will become easier over time, so you can improve considerably both at it and from it.

Improving Through Education

Education remains one of the best ways to improve your mind. It challenges you to think in different ways so that you gain greater knowledge and understanding. At school or in college, classes entail readings that provide information about the subject; lectures are carried out by well-educated professionals who explain concepts and answer questions; examinations find gaps in your understanding of the material; and class activities allow you to see how others are perceiving the same information.

These courses are created and reviewed by institutions to ensure a high standard of content for the student—textbooks are constantly being updated with new information when discovered. Professors are also often challenged by students during lectures, thereby learning from them each time they are asked to clarify or correct their teaching methods.

Learning from a course does have some advantages over self-study.

Where self-study is also self-guided, learning among others in a class exposes you to different viewpoints outside of your own. That being said, self-education does have its own advantages: It allows you to constantly explore and learn about what's important to you.

Taking classes can motivate you to learn as they typically require you to invest your time and money. It also offers incentive, because you can achieve a degree or other certifications that will support you in finding an interesting profession. Many new career opportunities become available through education.

Working can be one of the most undesirable things you have to do in your life. But, if you can find something you enjoy, perhaps that you access through education, it makes work more worthwhile. For these reasons, education and learning are worth it despite how difficult and time consuming it can be.

Improving Can Be Enjoyable

Improving the mind doesn't always have to be challenging. You can learn from many of the things you already enjoy doing. It may be surprising to know that games can improve the mind, too. There are games that improve your reaction speed, help build knowledge, and learn strategy.

You can improve your mind with board games, video games, and games that involve physical activity. Board games such as chess teach you to adopt a strategic mindset; games such as scramble, crosswords, and card games improve memory; video games such as first-person shooters help with hand-eye coordination; and real-time strategy games help you increase your response time, which can speed up decision making.

You have probably seen, or maybe have *been*, that person who caught something midair as it was falling to the ground, stopping it from shattering into countless pieces. It's likely this person is a video gamer, as playing these gradually improves response time. Games that require you to draw and act out certain things can improve also the creative parts of the mind.

If you play games early in the day, it can also give you a mental boost throughout the day.

You can gain additional benefits if you play games with other people. This gives you opportunities to learn new ideas and strategies to improve your tactics. Competitive games can motivate you to put in more effort, which leads to higher skill. Additionally, some games require you to work collectively with others, meaning you can develop your teamworking skills.

There are many ways you can find games to play with other people. Apps and computer games make it simple to meet other players online quickly and there are also many community groups that offer signups for card games, board games, and sports—or you can organize your own.

As previously mentioned, exercise can improve your mind because of its health benefits. Sports, like video games, are another great way to meet people and improve both the mind and body. You learn strategy, and improve dexterity, agility, and concentration, which makes you sharper and more energized during your day.

Improving Left- and Right-Brain Connections

You can also perform exercises focused on developing the connections between your left and right brain to greatly improve your mind. As mentioned earlier, you have a collection of nerve fibers that run between the two hemispheres of the cerebrum called the "corpus callosum." When you work on better developing this area of the brain, you can process information quicker—making you sharper with faster response times and the ability to make more accurate decisions.

Performing tasks that involve the use of both sides of your body can develop these connections. Switching up everyday things such as trying to write or use a computer mouse with your non-dominant hand is good practice and can be done often. Using both hands to type on a keyboard can also help—which is good, as this is often a necessary part of many people's days.

You could also learn to play an instrument that uses both hands while simultaneously learning or improving a skill.

Interpreters often have exceptionally developed connections between the left and right hemispheres of the brain because switching between languages is a very complex task. As such, learning a new language is an excellent way to improve your mind, and from it, you gain the ability to communicate with more people. It can also be very useful while traveling.

Juggling is often considered one of the best ways to develop your brain as it not only uses both hands, but also improves memory, focus, and hand-eye coordination.

As some of us use more of the left brain, and others more of the right, it's also beneficial to improve each hemisphere independently.

Those who are left-brained often have fantastic reasoning skills and are great at analytical tasks. Others that are right-brained often have amazing creative abilities. A creative person, in addition to performing the things they enjoy doing, may benefit from activities that require logic and reasoning to improve and balance their abilities. They could do this through reading more, answering riddles, or learning arithmetic problems.

Conversely, a person who is naturally good with logic and reasoning may benefit more from doing creative activities such as drawing or painting. The more you challenge your mind in different ways, especially ones that don't come easily to you, the more you will make considerable improvements.

It's quite remarkable when you achieve new things that were never before an interest to you because you were willing to try something different. You can develop many new and interesting skills because of your mind's ability to change and adapt to challenges.

Conclusion

Focusing on building a healthy and capable brain and mind allows you a platform to make any other improvements. Many of the ideas in this chapter can be added into your day so that you can slow mental decline and progress your mental state and skills. Though it's important to take breaks when you feel pressure and stress, it's equally important to challenge your mind, as this is how you improve it.

Just as exercise increases muscle mass, working the mind will develop it further. Good nutrition and avoiding harm to the brain will keep it healthy so that you can use it to the best of its ability. Reading and writing or taking a class are also great ways to improve your understanding and communication skills. Playing brain games is fun and improves your mind at the same time.

You have so many options to improve yourself and you may find that you enjoy the new skills you develop after making the effort to learn new things.

CHAPTER 2

Understanding Stress

As discussed in the last chapter, stress can be hard on the mind. Likewise, the different negative effects from stress can also extend throughout the body. The longer that stress continues unresolved or unmanaged, the more potential it has to cause harm. If you understand more about what stress is, and the manifestation of it in your body, you will be more likely to recognize when it occurs. Learning ways to detect and manage stress will allow you to address it quicker and more effectively.

Stress is prompted by stressors in your environment or thoughts in your head; there are triggers for it all around you. When you experience stress, your body secretes hormones to help you, such as cortisol and adrenaline—which increase your energy, focus, and immunity. However, this is intended to be an immediate aid for you to manage the stressor, or to get out of danger.

Though this physiological response is well equipped for short-term stress, it can tire if the stressor persists unaddressed, thereby losing its effect. Many of your thoughts and experiences keep you in this hyperaware state for a duration much longer than what the body can tolerate—this is when stress can begin to cause harm.

This chapter will explore deeper into the physiology of stress in your body, how you can identify it, and some great ways to manage it better to improve your ability to handle challenges more effectively.

Physiology of Stress

Many of us find it difficult to realize the extent of our stress, or even to identify when we're stressed in the first place. You may be too busy to notice, or perhaps just never consider its potential for harm.

Understanding the physiology of stress will allow you to perceive it within you when it occurs, understand what's causing it, and find ways to reduce its effects on you. When a stressor triggers you, your body automatically initiates a "stress response."

This is commonly described in three stages: The first is alarm. During this stage, the fight-or-flight mechanism is activated, and the brain signals the adrenal glands to secrete adrenaline into the blood stream. A wide range of responses then occur within the body: Pupils dilate, blood pressure rises, and heart and respiratory rates increase. The brain becomes hyperaware and your skeletal muscles contract and are primed to run or fight. Adrenaline also increases the amount of sugar in your blood stream to give you more energy, and your body temporarily loses homeostasis—the balance that it strives to maintain.

All these things combined give you an increased awareness of how to handle the challenging situation you've encountered. This can be very helpful if you need to run from a dangerous animal or handle an urgent problem. However, if it's triggered multiple times each day, or for prolonged durations, your body can begin to fatigue from this continuous state of alert.

Unfortunately, we allow this to happen frequently, and from trivial things, which can lead to health issues and difficulties handling any other problems that occur during our day.

Cortisol is another stress hormone released into the blood stream. This is intended to support or counter the shock phase so that your body returns to homeostasis. This is the next stage: The resistance phase, otherwise known as the adaption phase. In this phase, if homeostasis is achieved, the third phase can be delayed or even prevented. Symptoms are resolved and the body can begin to repair and replenish itself.

If the stressor is not adapted to, the body may go into the final stage: The exhaustion phase. Long periods of cortisol secretion can be harmful. This is typically brought on by persistent exposure to a stressor that the body has not recovered from. The energy produced during the adaptive stage is drained and no longer available; you may experience headaches, anxiety, depression, and decreased immunity. Furthermore, more serious problems can occur if there is no elimination or adaption to the stressor.

Short-Term Stress

This information about how our bodies react suggests that stressors should be addressed as quickly as possible, and our reaction to them should be managed as best we can. It may be helpful to assess how long a given stressful situation lasts.

Is it acute (a short-term stress lasting seconds, minutes, or hours)? Or is it chronic (a long-term stress continuing for days, months, or years)? An acute stress is something such as seeing a clump of lint move out of the corner of your eye and immediately thinking it's a spider.

Or perhaps it is a spider, and you're reaching for whatever weapon you can find nearby to defend yourself. This is typically a short-term stressor and can be handled quickly by addressing the perceived threat or leaving the area.

Another example of short-term stress is being late to work. You may panic and have racing thoughts until you meet your fate with your client or manager. This can be the extent of it; however, this can also advance into a long-term stress if you allow yourself to perseverate over it. It may not be the first time you're late, or you may be the type of person who takes being late very seriously, which can cause you to be quite hard on yourself. It's important to resolve or adapt to stressors as quickly as possible so that your body can resume homeostasis, and to reduce the chance of further side effects or health issues.

Long-Term Stress

Long-term stress and continued cortisol release can have many consequences for your health. It puts your body in a constant state of arousal that causes imbalance. Chronic stress can be brought on by more serious stressors, such as the loss of a loved one, moving to a new state, job loss, abuse, divorce, or financial difficulties. These difficult experiences can cause a stress response that lasts far longer, which puts strain on the body both physically and mentally.

Physical consequences of chronic stress can progress from small things, such as loss of energy and headaches, to more serious problems, such as high blood pressure, sleep problems, weight gain, heart disease, and more. Chronic stress can also lead to mental health disorders such as anxiety and depression.

An anxiety disorder may manifest from fear, nervousness, or tension because of the continued stress over the unknown. Depression may result from persistent sadness, regret, or hopelessness that is difficult to overcome. It's important to be able to identify stress and other negative feelings in your body so that you can determine appropriate ways to manage them.

Susceptibility to Stress

You can be more susceptible to stress because of reasons such as genetics, an excessively busy life, your mindset, a lack of organization, mental health conditions, poor nutrition and hydration, or inadequate sleep. Stress could also form easier when you're having a bad day—one of those where nothing seems to go right.

Our susceptibilities allow difficulties to build to the point of frustration and stress much faster. Learning strategies about how to organize and manage daily tasks that frequently diminish your time and lead to stress can help with this. Understanding mindset and how it effects your health, as well as ways to improve it can also help. Mental illness can be managed better by speaking to professionals and loved ones.

Proper nutrition is not only important for your health, but nutrient deficiencies can greatly impact how you feel and handle stress. Previously mentioned was the importance of sleep for the mind, but sleep also effects your energy, focus, and ability to handle problems. The coming chapters describe things that can make you more susceptible to stress as well as actual stressors so that you may identify them and manage them more effectively.

Stressors

In addition to your susceptibility to stress, you should also identify actual stressors—things provoke your stress levels. Most of us are aware of the things in our environment that trigger us easily, such as heat, or bad traffic on the way to work. These common stressors can be short-lasting and just need some patience, anticipation, and preparation to avoid them.

Unfortunately, there are greater stressors that have recurrent, longer-lasting effects that need more thought and attention to stop them from persisting.

Major stressors can be social, such as those from your relationships with people. This can be people close to you, such as family and friends, or it can be coworkers, business partners, or supervisors. Anyone we encounter can cause us stress as we are all very different from each other.

Another major stressor comes from financial difficulties, such as debt, low income, or having no savings. These two stressors involving relationships and financial problems are the top contributors to stress and will be discussed to a greater extent over the next two chapters.

Other common stressors that considerably provoke long-term stress are self-criticism, fears, loss, divorce, abuse, injury, and many others. We are all challenged so much throughout our lives. No one understands how you're feeling more than you do; the struggles that you face, the pain you feel, and the concerns you have about the people you care for.

You will encounter many troubles that require you to understand and problem-solve to settle them. We all do this in different ways naturally, but it's important to increase your understanding of what causes these problems to reduce stress and live healthier.

Having a Busy Schedule

Having a busy schedule can be a constant stressor and cause you to be more susceptible to other stressors. This can burden you greatly and leave little time for the fun that allows you to release stress.

You might be a very ambitious person and pack your day to accomplish as much as possible. You may also have many responsibilities that are difficult to keep up with. People can have little time to think about stress as they are always trying to accomplish more and more. If you then have responsibilities such as children, working, cleaning, cooking, or pets, then you likely have very little time to consider your own health and wellbeing.

While there are many great experiences and opportunities awaiting in life, it's sometimes necessary to slow down or limit responsibilities to achieve a good balance. Moreover, you should *listen* to your body and take breaks when you're feeling pressure, as this is your body *telling* you that you've taken on too much.

Good health is essential to your functioning, and you may find it even more difficult to manage your responsibilities or accomplish new things if your health and performance is compromised.

Organization

You can decrease stress and create extra time for yourself through using systems that improve your organization and planning. You may already do this, but there are always new strategies that can provide you with more time.

Organization sometimes involves letting go of things that you no longer have a use for, as this reduces the number of things you need to manage. It also makes space for the new things you wish to pursue. It can be difficult to let go of some of your things, but after removing them, there is much less to think about.

An effective method for achieving excellent organization is to create lists; they are exceptionally useful and will be mentioned in future chapters as well. Making lists can result in greatly improved organization and can prevent mistakes and missed opportunities. You can create lists for a wide range of aspects in your life.

WELL-ROUNDED

Imagine a to-do list, but one that is always evolving and includes things you have a propensity to forget or spend too much time thinking about. Making lists can be even more helpful if you organize them into categories. For example, you can have a "daily list" that includes things such as "exercise," "meditate," "read," and "review upcoming appointments and to-do-list."

Basically, anything you want to accomplish each day.

You can also have a "monthly list" that includes things such as "bills," "deep clean house and car," "make time-off plans," and so on—anything you want to be sure is done each month.

There are also "food lists," "travel lists" (places to go), "camping lists" (what to bring), "favorite restaurant lists," "goals lists," and many others.

It's helpful to have a notebook of these lists readily available so you can quickly decide when and what to do, rather than losing time thinking through your options and trying to remember. It's also important to grow these lists or reduce them over time for maximum efficiency. Making use of a planner for appointments or learning to use your smartphone for reminders and notes will also help you worry less and maximize your free time.

Changing Your Mindset

Too frequently, we let our everyday tasks get to us and cause untold amounts of stress—things such as irritating chores or work that is undesirable, difficult, or a burden on our time. A technique to help you deal with this is to try and see it not as a laborious task, but as a formidable, or even fun challenge. Perhaps by making it a game or competition of sorts.

Understanding Stress

In other words, persuading yourself to believe that it's not daunting or aggravating at all—that you enjoy doing it. You essentially trick your mind into thinking it's something you like doing, which can stop things from being stressors.

This may be difficult, but it can certainly work.
You can trick your mind and body into many things. You can overcome plateaus in fitness, discussed in a later chapter, and even convince your mind that you're enjoying things you typically wouldn't. This technique has been mastered by people in many different ways, making it a great method to explore and learn more about.

You will encounter many frustrating responsibilities that you must handle to avoid further problems, finding ways to enjoy them can reduce your stress considerably. People's attitudes toward tasks can vary widely; for example, some may dislike math, while others find joy in it. Ultimately, your mindset plays a crucial role in determining how stressful, tolerable, or enjoyable an activity becomes.

Positive Mindset Techniques

If you're having difficulties shifting your mindset, there are some methods that may help. Something that works well for many people is smiling every day; this is a powerful technique that can signal to your brain that you're in a good mood. It can also trigger the release of dopamine, endorphins, and serotonin. These hormones can relax your body, reduce stress, and improve how you feel.

Additionally, smiling is contagious, so it may cause others around you feel better too. Furthermore, it makes you more approachable, which creates more opportunities to engage with others. Try it and see if there's any improvement in your life. Another great way to decrease stress and improve your mindset is through random acts of kindness.

You may have heard about this before, but how do you help others?

A great way to find opportunities for this is by being aware of your surroundings and anticipating the needs of the people around you. This way, you can spot a chance to help someone with a problem, find something nice to say about someone's look, or see an opportunity to comment on someone's great performance.

These small things can change other people's mindset while also making you feel better. If the other person happened to be troubled about something, then the timing couldn't be better.

People love to hear compliments and have others notice their hard work—it can really make someone's day.

Negative Mindset

Your mindset can impact your health and levels of stress in ways that can be both beneficial and harmful. A negative mindset can make it difficult for your body to feel those positive emotions that are healthy and advantageous, and you may become predisposed to observing failure everywhere.

This may impede you from seeing solutions to your problems. Consequently, your troubles will worsen and persist for longer.

On the other hand, a positive mindset will aid you in difficult situations. Happiness and optimism are good feelings and attitudes that energize and shift you into a more constructive thinking pattern. Whether you have a positive or negative mindset, you may also have certain stress-inducing behaviors. Behaviors such as self-criticism and over-analyzing things can add a great deal of stress, which can be harmful when attempting to improve yourself.

Understanding Stress

Self-criticism leads to worry and negativity, which can make you feel like a failure or hopeless. You may believe that criticizing your actions is beneficial as it calls out your mistakes or dissatisfaction. But this is simply not true. Your mind connects negativity to your memories and knowledge. If you believe you're a failure at something and criticize yourself, your mind will believe you're less capable and will reduce your confidence when you try to do things in future.

Confidence is very significant to your energy and ability to do things well, so long as you do not allow yourself to be naïve or overextend yourself. A healthier and more constructive approach is self-reflection. This is where you identify any mistakes, think of ways that success can or could have been achieved, and then move forward. You can do this without blame or criticism; be aware of the mistake and understand that not everything can be anticipated beforehand.

It's also important to try your best to avoid over-analyzing things, which can cause the mind to fatigue under the excessive pressure to solve a problem. As mentioned before, you will benefit greatly from taking breaks when you start to feel imminent frustration. Breaks allow you to return to problems later with a fresher look. Having high standards is good—these are powerful motivators that let you accomplish great things—but some ways of upholding these are healthier than others.

Navigating Stress

This is by no means a complete list of stressors. You should always try to determine what in your life is causing you discomfort. You can identify stress or negative feelings on your own, or get feedback from a friend, family member, or practitioner.

There are many ways to improve your wellbeing. Countless people maintain very good lives despite experiencing stress and any other significant problems they have. There are established ways to address acute and chronic stress; it is even possible to reverse many of the long-term consequences caused by it. You may have some of your own ways that you've developed to cope with stress, as each of us experience it in different ways.

You don't have to do it alone, though.

Although it's not always easy to speak to others, you can learn from specialists or other people's experiences in order to find new answers and learn new ways to improve.

Searching for Answers

If your stress becomes too much to manage, or you experience mental or physical symptoms, it's a sign to search for answers.

It's most beneficial to begin with a doctor whenever you don't feel well, as they are the experts and have the most comprehensive knowledge and experience regarding how to address problems with the mind and body. They can do an assessment and run tests to determine whether your stress is caused, or perpetuated, by reasons such as physiological imbalances, anemia, nutrient deficiency, or mood disorders.

Their assessments and findings may give you some much-needed answers.

Your doctor can also suggest the latest treatments, recommend a nutritionist for deficiencies, a therapist for troubles with emotions, and so much more. It's relieving to find the source of your problems and understand ways to feel better. It is also important to understand that not all specialists will be right for you. This is true of any profession. It may be worth getting a second opinion to help you find the best practitioner for you. Yet, it should not discourage you from seeking answers and ways to improve. There are many great practitioners out there that can get you the answers you need.

Speaking to a doctor can get you answers and solutions quickly, which saves you time, distress, and helps you get back on track. In addition to seeing a doctor or other specialists, there are many other things you can do each day to ease stress.

Walking

Regular walking is a great way to reduce stress and it comes alongside many other health benefits. Sometimes, you can get caught up doing the same things each day; taking a small break to go for a walk will give you an escape and help you feel more relaxed. Moreover, walking can enhance blood flow to the brain, making it an effective means of mentally sorting through any problems.

Aristotle, a brilliant Greek philosopher, was known to walk during his lectures. He was recognized as a "peripatetic," meaning a person who learns as they walk. Many people find it easier to think and find inspiration when they are walking.

Walking in nature is even better; the scenery can be incredible and lively and there is typically less pollution and distraction.

Changing your regular walking route and visiting different areas can also help you get new experiences out of it. You can find places with waterfalls, rivers, animals, plants, and flowers. You can also experience fresh air, a variety of smells, and ambience, all of which are invigorating and helpful to your wellbeing.

Walking also makes you physically feel better as it releases endorphins.

Additionally, you can increase bone strength as your bones must acclimate to the force and pressure experienced when walking. Many muscles are used for walking, and they too will improve. Walking with others also provides additional benefits, such as improved communication skills, learning new ideas from others, and building emotional connections.

There is so much you can do to improve yourself and feel better if you find time to walk regularly.

Activities and Interactions

Many parts of this book will mention the health benefits of exercise. Still, you can maximize these benefits by exercising with other people. Many of the benefits of social interaction have already been mentioned and will be further discussed in the next chapter. However, a particular benefit regarding stress specifically is that you can learn new ways to manage your problems through exercising with others.

Exercising, or any activity with others, gives you an opportunity to talk to people about your difficulties and discuss any problems on your mind. You could be stressed about work, relationship issues, or a difficult decision you're struggling to make. The people you meet may have been in a similar situation and have a helpful solution for it, or they may at least listen to you and provide emotional support.

This can also be reciprocal, as you can listen to their concerns and may have ideas to help and support them with their problems. Sometimes, just knowing how difficult it is for others can help reduce self-criticism and the unrealistic expectations you place on yourself.

There are many ways that you can develop through socializing and being active. You can exercise with friends by asking them to join you the next time you plan to work out or go for a run or walk. This can help them with their health and stress too.

You can also join sports groups, which makes exercise more challenging and thrilling and gives you the opportunity to meet new people, make connections, and build relationships. Get started by searching for activities, clubs, or different events in your local area that look interesting. Or create your own if the area you live in doesn't have many to offer. This may be difficult in more remote areas, but it could be worth reaching out to people by posting signup sheets at the closest grocery store or restaurant.

Bonding with Pets

Pets have been found to help people decrease their stress. They also help people with depression, anxiety, and other mental health disorders. They are becoming increasingly allowed in public places to support people with disabilities and mental health problems; pets are welcome on some planes, and other places where you wouldn't normally think permittable. Often, certain places that don't allow pets make exceptions if the person has the proper documents, such as a doctor's note, stating their pet is an emotional support animal.

Pets make us happy: They are living, feeling beings that love you just as much as you love them. Many people have reduced their stress and developed strong bonds with their pets that help them feel loved and appreciated.

There are so many pets in all different shapes and sizes; try and find one that's right for you. Pets are also a responsibility—they require you to take care of them and to put their needs before your own from time to time. Having obligations such as these can help you strive for better structure in your life, encouraging you to be dependable, compassionate, and supportive.

Conversely, pets can also add stress to your life. They are not right for everyone, and you should take great care to understand whether they are right for you. Pets take a certain amount of patience, especially in the earlier stages of their life when they are young and make many mistakes as they develop good behaviors.

If you feel a pet is right for you, there are many that need homes and care in local shelters. Adopting from these both saves a life and finds you a great companion.

Hobbies

Many people successfully lower their stress levels by pursuing new hobbies.

There are many great hobbies, but one with extensive benefits for your stress and wellbeing is taking care of plants. This is yet another responsibility that requires you to learn more so that you can properly sustain the environment needed for your plants to thrive and grow. This maintenance adds more structure to your life, as ensuring this is crucial to keeping your plants alive.

In addition to reducing stress, taking care of plants outdoors or placing them around your home can lead to increased physical activity. Furthermore, the vibrant colors and invigorating smells of plants, along with the rewarding experience of watching them grow and flourish, contribute considerably to your mental health. Growing fruits and vegetables can also improve your health, as you can avoid buying chemically treated store-bought food. It can also save you money as seeds are a much lower expense than fresh produce.

Plants and flowers can also create an aesthetically appealing home and yard and improve indoor air quality. Many people have plants, or a garden they spend time tending to, which improves mood and reduces stress.

Meditation

You've likely heard that meditation is great for stress. You may even take advantage of this currently. Meditation is very helpful for the mind and body when done correctly and performed often. It can be difficult to find time and a quiet place to meditate, but if you can add it to your schedule, you can greatly improve your stress levels.

It may work best to meditate first thing in the morning and last thing before bed, as this is when things are typically the quietest. You may have to be very strategic to find opportunities to meditate, but it is well worth the effort. Even short moments away from your thoughts to close your eyes and take some deep breaths can help release a little pressure.

Closing your eyes is an important part of trying to meditate as it removes everything visual from the picture. After that, it's only your mind and remaining senses that are creating and perceiving information. When you commit to meditation, it's very important to try and clear your mind as best as possible. This can be very difficult, but you will improve over time if you meditate often.

One technique is to concentrate on your breathing: Breathe slowly and deeply. You must then try to avoid thinking. It may be easier to think about it like going on vacation. Usually, when you're on vacation, you're in a new place without access to all the things that keep you busy, which can really help you let go of everyday thoughts. Therefore, you typically feel more relaxed and open to new things.

These are just a couple of techniques that can clear your mind and help you relax enough to meditate effectively. There are many ways to enter a meditative state, and if you don't connect with one or another you can always search for new ones. If you continue having trouble by yourself, you can try attending a guided medication session. These can take place in person or at home—there are many convenient videos online that you can listen to.

Music

Many people already recognize that their stress and mood improve when they listen to music. That's because it's another way to release the hormones that make you feel good and improve your mindset. There are many different choices of music that can improve energy and focus—these can help you stay awake, exercise, improve concentration, or motivate you to do chores or other things that often get put on hold.

Some colleges allow their students to listen to music while testing as it can help them to focus better.

You can also try different types of music for sleep and relaxation. This can help you unwind and reduce the stress accumulated throughout the day. Music is also a great way to improve a negative mindset or help with sadness and disappointment. It can reduce difficult feelings so you can shift to more constructive thinking.

Whenever you feel stressed, putting on some music might be just what you need to improve your mood and be better engaged in your day.

Conclusion

Your body is well-equipped to handle small amounts of stress—it's continued stress that's harmful to your mind and body. It diminishes your energy and can lead to many adverse symptoms and health problems.

There will be many challenges that require you to problem solve and find ways to overcome them. Learning more about stress is helpful for

Understanding Stress

identifying it as soon as it occurs, and is crucial to supporting your well-being. This can make you more confident and productive, so you can focus on enjoying life and pursuing your interests.

CHAPTER 3

Establishing & Maintaining Relationships

In a world where the personality differences between human beings are so extensive, relationships are a common stress trigger. However, although this may be true at times, studies show that people live longer, healthier, and happier lives when they also have strong social bonds with others.

The relationships you have with family, and the connections you make out in the world, deeply impact who you are and who you will become. This is because you learn from each person you encounter in your life.

Improving your understanding of your emotions and impulses, and how these factors can provoke certain behaviors, may allow you to manage them better. It can also help you determine what may be motivating others to behave as they do.

This is useful when building relationships as it allows you to control your emotions and better understand another person's situation. You may experience many challenges when communicating with others because of your differences with them. You may need to adapt and be flexible at times, but you must also have boundaries and assert your limitations clearly. Equally, you may want to learn the limitations of others so as not to offend them.

These things will not always be apparent, as people will not always be forthright, but by improving your understanding of emotions, behaviors, and differences between people, you can improve your communication and ability to build quality relationships. It's important to understand that you yourself may be motivated to develop and give your best effort, but others may not do the same.

You have no control over other people and their desire to improve.

Developing your understanding will only allow *you* to read situations better so that you can communicate in a way that impacts conversations to achieve the desired outcome. In addition to understanding the sentiments of yourself and others, there are many useful approaches that may help you both maintain your current relationships and make new connections to aid in building new ones.

Our Differences

Your mind is a product of your genetics and the environment you grow in. From a genetic standpoint, your biological parents contribute twenty-three chromosomes each, allowing for an astonishing number of different combinations. Essentially, trillions of different babies can potentially be created by your parents. Therefore, you can be immensely different from your siblings, and very distinct from people birthed by other parents.

This is the first factor that determines why you think and feel differently than every other person on earth. Even in the event of identical twins who share the same chromosomes, they can have different genetics to some extent, if they modify. Furthermore, each twin will have different interactions with their environment after they are born.

This leads us to the second factor: Our environment.

Possibly while still in the womb, you start experiencing things and building memories that will form your personality over time. These two factors create many differences between people, so trying to understand each other can sometimes be difficult. You may relate to people in some ways—and have similar likes and dislikes—while also having many differences. This has resulted in the remarkable, diverse, and challenging world we live in.

Physiology of Emotional Connections

When it comes to maintaining relationships and forming new ones, your mind is constantly working to establish how people fit into your life—this understanding evolves the more you learn about them.

Your brain's limbic system is a collection of structures mainly responsible for this process.

Incidentally, this is the same system that activates the stress response discussed in the last chapter. The limbic system is made up of a few known parts; two of its structures are largely responsible for how you collect and utilize information to determine whether relationships are right for you now and in the future.

One of these main structures is the hippocampus, responsible for learning and memories. It allows you to store and retrieve memories created from your experiences. Another important function of the hippocampus is to connect these memories with your different senses, such as your sense of smell. For example, the smell of an evergreen tree may cause you to think about Christmas time.

The other main structure is the amygdala, which is responsible for your emotional responses. It triggers feelings of happiness, pleasure, fear, and anger and also decides the strength of your responses and attaches these emotions to memories.

Although this may be a universal process, we each feel and create memories in different ways because of our genetics and previous experiences. Furthermore, your emotions towards things can adjust over time as you are constantly changing due to the events in your life.

Emotional Responses Vary from Person to Person

The limbic system is consistently facilitating your emotions in unique ways that allow you to understand and react to experiences. Because of our differences, we all feel emotions in different ways and at various levels. This may cause confusion when another person responds differently than you do in a select circumstance.

For example: Two people approach a small bird, which lays deceased on the ground. One person might exhibit profound sadness and compassion, while the other may show no visible response, yet both may be affected internally, expressing their emotions in different ways.

This is one reason why communication can be so difficult; we all have different expectations and, if another person does not respond to a situation as you expect them to, you can become confused and disappointed. It doesn't necessarily mean the person cares less or isn't listening.

Another problem you might encounter is that your limbic system can work on a survival basis and focus on things that benefit your well-being. Therefore, your emotions may often be directed towards your interests first and foremost. This can make it difficult to see things from another's perspective. Additionally, emotions can initiate the fight-or-flight response discussed in the last chapter. This is a response that you have little control over, and its effects can cause a greater emotional response then you would like.

These distinct reasons add to the complexities of developing relationships and why learning about your emotions is useful. Understanding these factors may help you to acknowledge what is happening to yourself and others internally during interactions, and how your emotions can be significant influencers on the outcomes of these exchanges.

For example, when a person is angry, the limbic system, like the stress response, triggers the release of adrenaline and cortisol into the blood stream, resulting in the fight or flight response.

Although this would help you get to safety if you needed to, this response is not conducive during an interaction with someone, and it can drive people away or cause them to act irrationally. For instance, anger can overpower your mind's reasonable thinking capacity and cause poor decision-making. Therefore, learning to control emotions better is important to improving the environment for constructive communication.

You cannot control other people, but if you learn to control your own emotions, you will engage more productively and be less likely to exacerbate poor emotional reactions in others.

Cultivating Positive Emotions

Another emotion you can learn to understand better is happiness—as many health benefits result from this emotion. Cortisol levels decrease and feel-good hormones such as dopamine and serotonin release, which helps reduce stress and improve mood.

Therefore, frequent moments of happiness will improve health and longevity and allow you to be more productive, as your interest in doing things will be greater during periods of happiness. Furthermore, happiness can give you more confidence and make you appear more approachable, which helps when making connections with people.

It may be surprising to learn that there are also risks if you don't have control over this emotion. Sometimes, happiness can lead you to be gullible and misled. You may also take more risks if you become too confident and misjudge your capabilities. Additionally, extreme happiness may be seen as selfish as it can overshadow the people that you intend to build relationships with.

It's important that other people feel valued too if you wish to progress with them.

Risks of Emotional Suppression

Learning to understand and control your emotions does not mean that you should suppress them. It's important to express your emotions in a healthy way so that they can flow through you.

Sometimes, we don't allow ourselves the pleasure of happiness as we may see it as a celebration when we do not yet consider ourselves accomplished. But there are many health benefits that can be realized through experiencing this emotion. Happiness is a powerful feeling that can improve your health by lowering stress, and it's important for you to recognize your hard work and achievements, as it will improve your confidence and make you feel more capable.

Another frequently suppressed emotion is sadness. It can be difficult to express this emotion, especially when other people are present. We often neglect this emotion because it shows our vulnerabilities.

However, it is necessary to release and allow it to proceed through its course; your body will try to help you feel better by secreting serotonin. While you can eventually find coping mechanisms for your problems, suppressing your feelings in the meantime can cause a much greater emotional response later on.

There are many advantages to managing your emotions, but it's important to allow yourself to feel happy and accomplished, and to also feel and express your sadness. You must learn to do this without letting it influence your rational thinking and decision making.

Acknowledging Emotions in Others

Just as sadness is difficult to express, it may also be difficult to see in others. You may find it difficult to help people that are sad because it makes you uncomfortable, too. You may be dismissive or minimize their pain because you do not feel it yourself.

A common response is to offer logical solutions to try and ease the other person's pain, however this can also cause them to suppress their emotions if they are not given appropriate time to first understand their problem and the feelings that result from it. Moreover, your answer may not be the right one for that person. As already discussed, people are vastly different from each other. You don't know what's best for others, even if it seems logical to you; what another person feels is very different from what you feel.

An approach that may help is to show that you care by saying that you recognize that person's pain, and simply asking whether there is anything you can do to help. This shows that you acknowledge and care about their problem and are someone that they can talk to.

Asking them questions about their problem can be helpful because it can encourage them to reflect on it, which can help them think of solutions—ones that are meaningful to them. If you have a viable solution to their problem, you can simply ask them if they would find it useful, or if they have thought of it yet. Although it's important that you don't get offended if they choose not to act on it—your disappointment can add to their troubles.

You can be helpful if you have the patience to listen and reassure them that they can get through their troubles.

Emotions and Memory

Thus far has described some of the reactions that occur within you—reasons for why you may feel and express your emotions a certain way or to a certain extent, and how this is different for everyone. Additionally, we have covered that controlling your emotions can be beneficial so long as you don't neglect them altogether.

It was also stated that you can connect emotions to your memories. So, what kind of effect might this have on your mind?

Psychologically, your emotions and experiences are continuously making changes to your way of thinking. As discussed in the first chapter, your brain has neuroplasticity, which means it will constantly be changing and adapting to improve your knowledge and protect your mind and body. The emotions you feel, the thoughts you have, the joys and stresses you experience, every event that you internally and externally perceive is constantly altering your mind.

When you have a strong emotional response to something, you may create a stronger memory that can be recalled easily, even if you wish to forget it. Very likely, you will remember your worst day in far greater detail than your best day, even though they are both capable of creating a strong emotional memory.

This is yet again related to our survival as a species; we needed to remember threatening situations in order to avoid them, even if it was something we would likely never encounter again.

Emotional Disorders

Your mind is strong, but it also has vulnerabilities. Consequently, experiences of loss, abuse, and trauma can both physically and mentally trouble you for extended periods of time.

Traumatic events can also lead to serious mental health illnesses. As discussed in the mind chapter, your genetics decide how susceptible your mind is to different things—including what risks you may have for developing mental health disorders—but some extreme traumatic events can trigger this in almost anyone.

A mental illness is characterized by irregularities in mood, thinking, and behavior. Developing these disorders will cause you to have difficulties controlling your emotions and living a balanced life. Many who have these disorders often feel depressed and down, or anxious and worried.

You might also have uncontrolled feelings of fear and anger, and negative thoughts that make your life difficult. It can affect how well you manage challenges, and your ability to build and maintain relationships with others.

A large percentage of adults worldwide have some type of mental health disorder. Many live their lives relatively well with these, but others struggle considerably. Mental illness is not chosen, and no one wishes it upon themselves.

If you look at this promisingly, because mental health disorders are so common, doctors and therapists have a great understanding of how to treat them successfully. There are many natural and medicinal therapies that can stabilize these types of illnesses, giving people the opportunity to enjoy their life and form healthy and lifelong relationships with others.

If you have someone in your life that opens up to you about their mental illness, it's important that you do not use that against them when there is a break in communication. If you truly care about that person and want to strive for a healthy relationship with them, you must be patient and try to communicate constructively. Learning more about their disorder and asking them about what you can do to help may improve your understanding of how to be compassionate and supportive.

You are not leaning how to diagnose, treat, or counsel them; you're learning how to listen and better understand them, how to communicate with them better, and how to recognize when they are at risk. The intention is to always improve yourself—in doing so, others may observe your conduct and aim to improve themselves, too.

In cases like this, you're helping a person with complex challenges and becoming someone they can have as support as they work to improve themselves.

Behavioral Development

Even without mental health disorders, everyone exhibits different behaviors from others. You have unique perceptions and beliefs about what you think is appropriate or not. Making and maintaining relationships is difficult when we all understand and feel things differently.

Meeting new people challenges you to modify your behaviors, at least to some extent, to maintain a relationship with them long-term. The things you have in common with others establishes a base for the relationship, but beyond that you may need to make some adjustments to your beliefs or actions to sustain it long-term.

This has been explained by Austrian neurologist Sigmund Freud as the superego.

Establishing & Maintaining Relationships

Your superego develops from your experiences with others; you see how *they* behave and compare it with how *you* behave. You may then make changes to your beliefs and behaviors after different types of experiences. Your parents or teachers may tell you something is inappropriate, and if it makes sense to you, you'll make the change to your behavior.

You may also make the change out of fear of being corrected again. Sometimes, observing others getting criticized for their behavior can motivate you to change as well.

Additionally, you may change to be close to someone you care deeply for. These are all ways that may challenge you to consider changing your behaviors and beliefs if you so choose to be affected by them. You may not realize it, but you can influence change in others, too.

Your perceivable behaviors—such as when you share your opinions, give feedback, or act a certain way—may cause others to change. You do not have to make changes to your beliefs if that isn't right for you; equally, you should not impose your beliefs on others if they do not agree, no matter how compelling your view is.

Each person should be free to determine their own beliefs.

You are not required to make any changes to your beliefs, but if you allow yourself to be open-minded, you can learn and improve yourself greatly with new information.

That said, it is essential to be at least somewhat skeptical of the things you see and hear. It can benefit you to substantiate questionable assertions from others, as misinformation will be presented often.

Discerning new information to determine its credibility will help you build a robust belief system that will provide you better judgement and better protect you from being misled. You can then share your well-vetted beliefs with others and convey more useful information.

Although this can improve you as an individual, it doesn't make developing relationships that much easier. Truly, if you want certain relationships to last, you must be patient and work on communication. Each person should feel seen, heard, and valued in a relationship.

Relationship Difficulties

When communication becomes difficult, it's important to take breaks, as this allows time for people to organize their thoughts, further consider the information from the other party, and determine their next actions more carefully.

As discussed previously, decision-making is less rational when you're upset. If you have made many attempts and things just seem to go nowhere, it may mean that you have quite a different understanding from this other person. Some relationships are unsustainable because you're incompatible with someone, so it may be sensible to limit your contact with them.

While sincere efforts can be made to improve a relationship, some have the potential to be detrimental to your well-being, making it essential for your health and happiness to consider ending the relationship. People's forgiving nature can complicate this decision, potentially allowing it to proceed to a point of harm.

Ending Unhealthy Relationships

You should end a relationship if it becomes unhealthy for you to continue it. You may not always be able to create effective communication in a relationship, or the other person may not be as determined as you are for a good outcome.

Then, at what point does it become important to let go of a relationship?

Establishing & Maintaining Relationships

Discussed earlier, people you care about may have mental health illnesses and need you to be a good, supportive listener as they can become emotionally unstable at times. In these situations, you can learn to adapt and make these relationships last without it becoming harmful to you if you're able to remain stable and involved.

But what about narcissists and antisocial people that tend to be toxic in relationships?

These are personality types that historically take advantage of people, mostly without realizing it. Not all people with these personality types will be difficult people, and people don't need to have a personality disorder to be a bad fit for you. It becomes clear and necessary that a relationship is unhealthy when someone causes you emotional or physical pain. It can then be a prudent decision to limit your time with them or end things completely.

Improving Communication

You can further improve yourself through pursuing and maintaining healthy relationships that allow you to learn from others. You do not have control over other people, but there are many things that you can do to encourage good relationships.

Previously stated, it's important to establish effective communication and to have a certain amount of patience. Regarding communication, people cannot read minds. Therefore, it's important for you to explain what you're thinking, especially to people you know well as they trust you not to mislead them. In doing this, you can describe what's bothering you in more detail so that they may better understand what you want them to know.

This can prevent people from making the sorts of assumptions that lead to miscommunication. Likewise, you can also avoid making your own assumptions by asking people questions when clarification is needed, or when their expressions don't suggest you understand their objectives.

Making assumptions can also lead people to believe the other person's overall objectives will be of no use to them before they have communicated it entirely. They may then cut the other person off before they are able to make their point. This can result in a break in communication, offensive behavior, and pushing people away. Avoiding assumptions can allow people to feel heard and may reveal a valid point from which you can learn something.

Improving these areas of communication can reduce speculation and misunderstandings, and the stress that often follows.

It also helps to explain your position and to ask questions to get as much information out in the open as possible. You want to fully understand each side of a disagreement.

Focusing on current issues is also important because irrelevant matters often become the main points of disagreement—someone may try to use unrelated issues to support their position without merit. Additionally, you can ask people to repeat illogical statements so they can hear themselves speak it again. They may better clarify themselves the second time around.

Ultimately, you may not agree with each other, but if you have enough information to make a more reliable decision, you can rest assured that you're making the best one you can. It may eventually become necessary to just move on with your differences. Simply telling someone that you don't agree can show them how firm you are with your decision.

You can end many disagreements by confirming your position and recognizing the other person's as well.

Patience

Patience is also important due to the differences between people.

When a disagreement *does* transpire, it's important for you to remain calm and control your emotions. Getting upset will lessen your ability for constructive discussion and can initiate or exacerbate irrational behaviors in others. If the other person does get upset, keeping calm can bring them back to an even temper.

It can initially cause them to be more upset when they see you so calm, because they may want you to engage with their intensity—they may even use personal attacks or false claims to trigger you into acting out. But if you disregard their attempts, they may notice that they are the only one acting irrational. It can then become more difficult for the person to justify their dramatic behavior to themselves.

This can help you to establish a less emotionally-driven discussion.

Establishing New Relationships

There is so much benefit to be found in establishing good relationships with people. Creating new relationships allows you to network and make new contacts, form emotional bonds, and learn considerably.

Networking will allow you to exchange ideas that can improve the success of both parties. Making new friendships with people helps you enjoy life and form a support system. You can also search for love and companionship, which can help you reach the deepest of emotions.

Although there are many challenges to consider with new relationships, they can be overcome. Many of us are very busy, so giving your time to others may be difficult. Additionally, you may not want people in your life whose goals do not align with your own. Consequently, you may need to focus on the relationships that are best for you.

Being approachable is the first step to permitting people into your life: You must be easy to connect with. To start with, you could focus on common interests and physical attraction, as they are typical foundations. Initially, it's sensible to set some boundaries, but you should avoid judging new people completely from your past experiences.

Everyone is different and will likely be nothing like anyone you have previously met. This is a time to build trust and try to understand why this person wants you in their life, and why you want to know them. It is also important to be upfront about who you are and what your intentions are to reduce the chance of any future miscommunications.

People want honesty so they can make choices right for them. If you let others know who you are, and try to understand them, you can develop life-long relationships with those you respect and appreciate.

Relationships Without Similarities

Often, we come together with people that we don't have much in common with. This typically happens when we go to work or school. You may find it challenging to make connections with some of these people because they don't share similar interests with you, you just see them often.

You may be left with little choice but to work with them and get through your differences. However, although you may not see yourself ever finding common interests, you can still learn a lot from the people who are the least like you. Situations like this can confront you with considerably different perspectives and new ideas.

In the workplace, the environment can be very competitive, and building relationships with people here may be even more difficult. As with all relationships, you must build trust while knowing there is always

Establishing & Maintaining Relationships

potential for someone to abuse it. In this case you can simply limit what people know about you and build from there.

Yet again, controlling your emotions is crucial; being able to think clearly allows you to take more calculated actions when doing business with others. Your biggest opportunity to meet new people is at work or school, so being completely guarded here will diminish your chances of new relationships.

Understanding New People

Establishing new relationships can be challenging because you don't know anything about the other person yet. You don't know how they perceive you and what their expectations are.

It's generally recommended to be yourself and act natural, but most people will want to adjust in some way to make things more comfortable and improve communication. Learning to read people can help you communicate with others better in the beginning.

As mentioned before, you cannot read minds, but you can learn to read people's behavior to try and deduce their intentions. This can cause problems with your established relationships because people may get offended or be less open with you, so it may be better to simply ask them what's on their mind.

New people will likely be less comfortable with sharing things. Therefore, developing your ability to read them makes sense for many reasons. You first need to know if you can trust them if you wish to share information about yourself and try to develop a relationship with them. You also want to know whether they have similar interests or goals and want to find any reasons for making any further effort to build the connection.

In a business setting, if your goal is to market to them or their company, you may want to read them as much as possible so you can keep them engaged with your ideas. A great method for doing this is allowing people to speak as much as possible and by asking them many questions. This will give you a multitude of information about them that will help you identify their character and style.

Another tactic is to watch their behavior; this will give you clues as to what motivates them. The more effort they put into something, the more passionate they are about it. Their actions are also indications of what they may be deciding internally. For example, if they are backing away, they probably don't like an idea or need to think about it another way; if they are leaning in, they are likely engaged and anticipating more information.

Certain people are very good at reading others as they create many opportunities to practice and improve this skill, which lets them develop a sense for it. Observing people and making predictions frequently can help you to develop this skill. Learning to read people allows you to understand others' intentions, improve communication, and provides you more opportunities to connect and learn.

Starting Conversations

One of the most difficult things about forming new relationships is getting the conversation started. It's hard to tell whether people are going to accept you if you try to talk to them, but if you don't try, you will have fewer opportunities in future.

Everyone has many experiences and ideas that they can share and talk about, but how do you get a conversation started?

One way to do this is by learning from individuals who are naturally good at it. There are people who are quite chatty and are great at forming relationships with others. These people are considered to have the "gift of gab."

But how do they do this exactly?

What typically happens is they just say *something*, anything that comes to mind. It may be something that happened last week, or it could have happened to them twenty years ago. It may have relevance to the situation, or it may have no relevance whatsoever—just stories or random pieces of information.

Whatever it is, they use it to initiate a conversation with someone.

Supposing this is the case, then, perhaps you could do the same. Assume that it won't be easy starting out, but if you push yourself out of your comfort zone, you can increase your chances of meeting new people. You can attempt this by saying something fitting, or even arbitrary, to anyone you might want to talk to, and then see how it goes.

You could try complimenting them, or point out something you notice in the general area. The argument being: Just say anything at all. Asking questions also works well; this will prompt them to speak, which gives you the opportunity to sense what they might be like.

From there, a common interest may present itself which can lead to further conversation. If it doesn't go well the first time, you may get better results the next time. It's likely you will not only experience busy and distracted people, but will also see some irritability and rejection.

But you don't need to take it too personally, they just may not be up for conversation. Nevertheless, initiating new conversations with people can provide great opportunities to learn from others and form new and interesting relationships.

Maintaining Current Relationships

Maintaining current relationships is also very important so that you can hold on to them. If you neglect your established relationships, you may lose important people in your life. You may not even know how much they really mean to you until they're gone.

Therefore, give the people currently in your life as much time as you can afford to. Once again, we can be very busy people, and managing your time for success and other aspirations can leave you with few opportunities to cultivate relationships with family and friends. But if you want these people in your life, it's essential.

Periodically reach out to check in on people. A short phone call can go a long way to stay connected with a friend or family member. Scheduling or accepting an invite to events and gatherings can give you more personal interactions with people; this will let you learn about what's happening in their life so you can appreciate what they have done recently.

You can also share your experiences and what new things have happened in your life. Within your intimate relationships, ask how their day was or give them a compliment. The more you stay engaged with people, the better you can sustain your relationships with them.

Parents and Siblings

Parents and siblings can often be your most fortunate relationships; many people have great relationships with the family they grew up with. You have normally gone through the most difficult learning stages of your life with them and needed each other to get through the worst of experiences.

Establishing & Maintaining Relationships

That being said, unfortunately, not all families thrive together. For instance, you are often your most natural self around them and say things more directly and with less of a filter. You know how to trigger and test your family, and they you. You might be competitive with your siblings and strive to be different from your parents.

Additionally, you may make assumptions about them, expecting your family to always be the same as you remember. As a result, you don't always acknowledge their growth and accomplishments. But people do grow and change; you are different now then you were a few years, or even a few days ago.

It would be unfair not to recognize their development by focusing too firmly on past behavior and therefore miss any improvements. Family often requires you to have patience due to the significant time spent with them as your most natural self.

If problems occur that do push you apart from family, you should really consider if it merits long or permanent periods of separation. Maybe the issue is rather trivial, something that can be resolved with a little understanding and communication.

If you have family, it's difficult to know what it would be like without them.

There are many people that have never experienced this type of bond, people that would dream of having a family like the one many of us neglect. So, if the problems you have are minor, then it may serve you well to find ways to restore these relationships.

Friendships

Some of the best relationships you will build in your lifetime will be with your friends.

These connections can be very meaningful.

Friends are who you share adventures with and who you may first look to for an opinion. They often greatly influence our personalities as they're typically first to offer criticism about the behaviors and beliefs we develop growing up.

You may often take your friends' comments as feedback, because you value their opinions and want to fit in with them. Everyone has different experiences, and friends will often challenge one another—but true friends also go to great lengths for one another.

Some problems friends have is when they make big life changes; for example, one friend may get married and have children, and another may move out of state for college. This can cause a shift in goals and activities—you may no longer align with goals of your friends'. New responsibilities mean change.

However, if you learn to balance your life and appreciate your friendships, you can hold on to people that you really trust and enjoy spending time with.

Another difficulty stems from misunderstandings and major mistakes in judgement. As humans, we are all fallible beings, and your choices are not always well thought through. Taking ownership and asking for forgiveness are genuine ways you can repair friendships.

If mistakes are not too significant, and you put effort into maintaining your friendships, you will always have someone there to look forward to seeing, to reminisce with about your past, and someone to create new adventures and experiences with going forward.

Significant Others

Your significant other also has a considerable impact on your health and wellbeing.

You unite with them because of your similarities and physical attraction and you often have a powerful drive to be with them. You invite them into your life, share your deepest thoughts and emotions with them, and they frequently see you at your most vulnerable state.

Some people enter relationships because they have a great deal in common with one another. Remarkably, others in romantic relationships may have little to nothing in common yet are driven together because of their intense love and attraction.

These forms of relationship can have a great impact on your mind and body. It's common to give so much of yourself to your partner that you can't imagine a world without them. Therefore, because it's such a profound emotional experience, it can leave you very hurt if ever separated.

People are so different from one another and are always changing; it is possible for you, your partner, or both of you to see each other in different ways over time. You may not feel appreciated, or your goals may no longer align.

Alternatively, personality differences can create tensions that accumulate to the extent that physical attraction and common interests no longer sustain the relationship. For many reasons, the person who was once the center of your world may no longer be right for you.

Previously discussed are the many ways you can work on communication—through acknowledging others and controlling your emotions. For struggling relationships, you can take things further by seeing a therapist.

Their objective opinions are great at explaining the differences between people, which will help you better understand both sides. Not all therapists are good at their profession; as with any, if one therapist can't help, it is possible that another may.

If you still care deeply for each other, there is potential for both people to improve and better contribute to the other. This may help the relationship to go on just as it once was, or even stronger. However, it's necessary to acknowledge that an unsustainable relationship can cause great harm through stress and unhappiness.

Although initially difficult, many people live better lives after a separation. The tension begins to fade, and many new possibilities present.

Children

A great way to improve yourself and feel more fulfilled in life is to form great relationships with your children. It is also essential for children to have strong bonds with their parents for their own health and understanding.

Not everyone has children, or ever will have them. Many people decide children are not right for them and enjoy different life interests—they may value many other things that grow themselves as people and form great relationships throughout their life.

Some take on the responsibility of animals, such as a dog or cat, and have love and compassion for them.

Sadly, some want children and cannot have them for numerous reasons. As a result, they search for ways to cope with the disappointment of this, and may find alternative ways to fill that wish, such as adopting, or volunteering their time with others.

But, if you have the opportunity, having children can really develop you as a person in a unique and powerful way.

Establishing & Maintaining Relationships

It adds great responsibility into your life as you have living and growing individuals that depend on you for their physical and emotional wellbeing. You have an obligation and responsibility to protect and care for them, because your decisions are what initiated their presence into the world. It becomes natural to begin considering their needs before your own; this changes your mentality.

Watching a child grow and develop is an amazing, remarkable thing to see. Their energy is inspiring, and their developing minds intriguing. Regrettably, life often becomes so busy that we lose valuable time with them, time we will never get back.

There is no way to reset the clock and start over. Therefore, it's important to spend as much time as you can building great bonds with your children, so they grow to appreciate you and feel loved.

Raising children is very difficult, and many mistakes will be made along the way. You will need to constantly adapt your parenting methods, because children are always changing—this requires you to change with them. Maintaining good relationship with anyone is difficult, and it is the same with your own children.

Yet, there are many things you can do to build strong relationships with them.

And it begins with your time: Give your children time when you are focused only on them, and they are not seen as a distraction. This allows you to understand their concerns and give them well-thought-out answers.

Being dismissive and giving empty responses gives children little to learn from.

A well-conceived answer, on the other hand, gives them the knowledge that you've developed over your lifetime. Additionally, children benefit from thorough explanations for why they cannot do something. There are likely very good reasons for certain limitations and an explanation will provide them more knowledge and understanding.

Communication can therefore improve your relationship with your children because they will feel more comfortable talking to you.

It also helps to ask your children questions, as this will challenge their minds. Asking questions is a very powerful method to help them build new neural connections, because they are accessing memories and devising responses.

One especially valuable time to ask questions is when they are angry, sad, or unhappy. This encourages them to use reasoning skills while in an emotional state. If you help them shift their attention to thinking and rationalizing, they may no longer give their emotions full control. This may help them begin problem solving through their feelings as well as help them realize that someone is there listening and caring about their problem.

Another great way to build relationships with children is to frequently teach them about different things. You can also include them in certain projects or hobbies you're working on. By becoming a constant source of information for them, they will associate you with their ability to learn. One of the most enjoyable ways to connect with your children is to do fun things with them. Taking them to new places and traveling, for example, are great opportunities to create new experiences and joyful memories with your children.

The most invaluable thing you can give your children is your time.

Conclusion

Forming and maintaining good relationships with people can be difficult. Allowing new people into your life requires learning and adjustment; your current relationships could be going very well one day, and the next you're perplexed to how they even began.

Although these challenges exist, you can improve the environment in relationships with good communication, by recognizing others, patience, and through managing your emotions.

You cannot control others, but if you improve yourself, you can promote more constructive interactions. Relationships are very important to your health, so you will benefit greatly from cultivating them to last. Conversely, poor relationships are harmful for everyone involved, so being realistic about their ability to continue is essential.

Having many good relationships shows your development as a person and is beneficial to your wellbeing.

CHAPTER 4

Financial Understanding

As previously mentioned, a person's financial situation can be yet another considerable contributor to their stress. Therefore, it makes sense that building your financial understanding will help you live a healthier life. It can also lead to better welfare overall if you make conscientious decisions that increase your time and ability to do the things you enjoy. It's easy for financial troubles to develop earlier in life before you've had many experiences. If you don't have a good mentor or someone to teach you how to manage money, you may have to learn from your mistakes.

Most people want to be successful in life, and this means something different to each of us. For one person it may mean a house, family, and vacations. Another person may want to travel across the country in an RV. And for someone else: A penthouse in New York City.

These are referred to as your life aspirations.

You may be driven to accomplish them, or they might simply be dreams for you to mentally escape to. The difference between being able to achieve your ambitions and them being unreachable desires is your plan on how to get there.

Planning requires a goal, something that your strategy can be designed to achieve. It requires clear objectives and for you to adapt them when you learn new information. You also need drive and a strong desire to reach them. And you should also have realistic expectations, so that you don't pressure yourself to the point you stop pursuing your goals.

There are many ways you can increase your financial understanding to remove debt and build savings. If you wish to be successful, you can do so by continuing to learn and improve.

Establishing Goals

Establishing your future goals is natural to do at some point, but there are stages in life when you may not be sure what you want yet. Many young adults tend to be apathetic about setting goals until they gain their independence and have experienced managing their life for a while.

Yet, at some point, life's experiences cause many people to shift their mindset and change their behaviors from pursuing instant desires, to considering a more calculated plan that involves their future.

If you choose to make this shift, you can set yourself up very well by improving your financial understanding and setting goals.

Your goals should have attainable timelines so as not to dissuade you. Timelines may also need to be adjusted over time in response to new information and unexpected changes in your life. It is possible to reach a goal much later than predicted; therefore, it's likely that you will have to modify your plans and expectations to make sure you stay on-course.

Financial Understanding

If reaching a goal is too challenging, you can try setting a smaller goal that's more attainable. Micro-goals are a great way to keep focused and make progress toward your bigger goals. If you understand that challenges are inevitable, and that not everything can be accurately deduced beforehand, you will be less discouraged when obstacles arise. Nevertheless, with organization and effort, you can achieve many great things.

It's also very possible to sometimes reach your goals much sooner than anticipated. Perhaps a better paying career presents itself and there is greater means to work with. This can allow you more options and may inspire you to make new goals to achieve even greater things than previously aspired to.

In contrast, you may reach your goals much later, or not at all. It's perfectly fine to push goals further away when you need to address important things that come up so long as you then get back to them when circumstances are more ideal.

Sometimes, life changes mean you have to let go of your goals—this is a common with divorce and breakups. During a relationship, you work with your partner to achieve the goals you made together. But once you're no longer together, you often feel lost and unsure of what you really want for yourself. It may take some time before you know what you'd like to do next, but it's beneficial to find something new to work towards.

Success is achieving your goals no matter what they are—and goals can change at any time.

Money Management

Once you have decided what you want to accomplish, it's important to set yourself up for a probable outcome. This requires you to first make a budget; a budget is the most helpful tool when planning. It gives you maximum control over your funds because it gives you perspective and allows you to set limits.

You can start by writing down all your bills, plus an allowance for gas, food, expenses, and entertainment. List these items in the budget and add them to the total. To progress towards your goals, you must make sure to write your total budget as far below your net income as possible.

This is called living below your means; the further you live below your means, the sooner you can reach your goals. If this is currently not possible, you will need to either increase income or decrease items in your budget.

Some ways you could increase income are by: Getting a new job, finding a side job, or starting a small business. If it isn't possible for you to find extra work outside the home, try looking online for remote jobs. Reducing the costs listed in the budget works, too. Many expenses are less beneficial than living below your means.

Some ways you could reduce these costs include making coffee and lunches at home; these two expenses have a surprising burden on your finances. Additionally, you could quit poor habits such as smoking and drinking alcohol, which not only decreases expenses but improves your health.

You can also bring drinks with you from home—gas stations and convenient stores are traps for unexpected spending.

Temporarily moving to lower cost housing or downscaling your vehicle can also really help.

Basically, you need move backwards in order to eventually move forwards. By lowering your budget and living below your means, you will create an excess of funds each month to pursue your dreams. It may be

Financial Understanding

surprising to learn that it is very feasible for a person making fifty-thousand dollars a year to pay off more debt and save more money than a person with similar circumstances making eight-thousand, or even one-hundred-thousand dollars a year.

A good plan is all that it takes to progress towards your goals.

Emergency Funds

Once you have control over your finances it's important to build savings for unexpected expenses. This will be different for each person, but one or two thousand dollars is a good start to address most unforeseen things. The reason for this is that you want to be able to pay for any unexpected expenses (such as your car breaking down) right away. This helps avoid the need to take out a loan—which may have high interest—or borrow from others.

Building your savings up too much can seem unfavorable, as inflation will reduce the purchasing power of your money over time. However, there are many people that don't take any risks and put all their extra money in savings, which works very well for them.

Debt

Once a small savings is established, begin paying off the debt with the highest interest rates first. Interest on loans is like giving free money to the bank. This could be extended to interest paid on motor vehicle loans too, as this will allow you to live further below your means and create more excess funds each month.

Paying off debt will allow you to remove financial stress and proceed more quickly towards your goals. Keep in mind that borrowing should be avoided as much as possible because interest is in addition to purchase price, which creates additional liability.

If you're having troubles addressing debt, there are many professionals who can help you. They can assist you in dealing with this burden much quicker, and often at a lower cost.

There are many different options you can look at for debt support. Debt repair companies have extensive experience helping people eliminate their debt and build their credit back very quickly. This can be a great way to go if you're looking to buy a home soon, or would just be happier seeing your credit higher but are not sure how to go about it.

Debt consolidation loans are also very helpful. They put all your debts into one single payment—often with a better interest rate—allowing you to pay off the total sooner, and at a lower cost.

Debt counselors can help you make an effective plan to finalize your debt and build a solid foundation of knowledge for managing money in the future.

All these options will likely come at some expense, but if you do the math, their service cost is trivial in comparison to what they can offer: They will help you remove your debt quicker, build your credit faster, and pay less. Always make sure to vet a company's reputation before choosing a service; there are many scammers and incompetent professionals that can make things worse. However, you should never underestimate the ability that professionals have to help you address your problems quickly.

This is what they have experience in.

If you are determined to do it yourself, there are many ways to research how to address debt and build credit. Once you're living below your means and have the funds to start improving things, it's time to address debt, raise your credit rate, and then move onto other things.

Financial Understanding

Savings and Inflation

It's an incredibly relieving feeling to be debt-free and build extra savings; pressure and stress levels lower considerably. You work very hard for what you have, you don't need to lose so much paying interest rates.

When the debt is gone, if you continue to live below your means, all that extra money can start building in your accounts. This allows you to build greater savings and progress even faster toward your goals.

Many different possibilities become available at this point, so building your financial awareness is highly valuable. One great way to add a little more to savings is to apply for a cash back credit card. It's easier to qualify when your debt is cleared, and your credit rating increases.

If you continue following your budget and pay off your credit card every month, you will get cash back on purchases you planned to buy anyways. However, it's important to keep in mind that it's also a temptation to use credit for unneeded purchases that deter you from your goals. If used strategically though, this method can add a good amount to your savings.

Historically, rising inflation will depreciate the buying power of your savings as you grow it. Therefore, it's helpful to build a thorough financial understanding to improve your decision making.

There are many ways to fight inflation, but most of them will involve some risk.

Investing in Yourself

Investing in the stock market can be a great way to combat inflation and even grow wealth. But this type of investing takes a great deal of learning and experience to do well. The markets are extremely unpredictable and require both risk and knowledge. Therefore, before investing in marketplaces, consider investing in yourself.

Investing your money and time to get a degree, certification, or apprenticeship can boost your pay considerably. You not only have the potential for greater income, but you may find something you enjoy doing. Additionally, you can feel proud about this accomplishment and what you have learned to get there. A career you like doing can make a substantial impact on your stress and make it easier for you to keep working for longer. Long-term employment with companies often results in more benefits, as well as possibilities for promotion.

Another option: If you have a business, or plan to start one, think about putting more money back into your business to grow it bigger and more profitable.

A business allows you to work independently and build something you can be proud of. However, it often consists of risk and long hours—which can result in considerable stress. Many business owners do a great deal of the work themselves because they want to protect their investment and reputation. If they learn new ways to spread out some of this work to others, they can reduce some of the pressure and free up more time to grow their company and do other things. Investing back into their business can result in less work and lead to higher profits.

Many people invest in places they have little or no experience in, and are then disappointed when their investments yield no returns. Investing in yourself gives you the ability and experience to scale what you know and understand.

Financial Understanding

Company Benefits and Long-Term Investment Strategies

A 401(k) plan, employer-sponsored retirement plan, IRA, or individual retirement plan are great ways to get some market exposure and build experience with different equities, such as index funds, small and large-cap funds, real estate funds, and mutual funds. Employers typically vet the funds they make available beforehand so they are ones that are widely used.

Additionally, these investments are normally highly managed mutual funds, or index funds that, to some extent, are already diversified. It's important to have a well-diversified portfolio because if one asset class does poorly, it's less likely to affect the entire portfolio. Retirement plans also build over a long period of time so there's no need to try and time the market with your contributions. If the overall markets historically do well over the long-term, then you can predict it will continue to do so going forward. However, retirement plans do have risks and should be considered carefully and with the aid of a financial advisor.

As a benefit, some companies offer matching or profit sharing for their employees. This is like extra money you can take advantage of when you contribute. It's important that you ask whether your company has a vesting schedule that requires you to stay with the company a certain number of years to receive the full amount the employer contributes to the plan. Another great benefit for starting a retirement plan is you can grow your account tax free if you hold it until a specific age, and then only pay taxes on the withdraws after.

Also, contributing to a 401(k) decreases your taxable income, so you may pay less in income taxes for that year. If you would rather not have the responsibility of actively managing your portfolio, there are targeted retirement funds that automatically reduce your risk as you near your desired retirement age. This will allow you significantly less risk in the event of a market crash around the time your retirement.

IRAs, also have many advantages. These are sometimes offered as an alternative through your employer, or you can set one up on your own to receive the benefits of both a 401(k) and IRA. There are many types of IRAs that let you into a lower tax bracket either now, or at retirement.

Bear in mind, because there are different types of IRAs, there are benefits and limitations for each. It also takes some forecasting to choose the right accounts, but fortunately, there are many financial advisors that can help you plan strategically. Many people set themselves up very well by planning for retirement as early as possible.

Retail Investing

Just about anyone can open an individual brokerage account and trade stocks that risk their capital for potential gains. This is referred to as "retail trading," but unfortunately, less than ten percent of these traders make money doing this.

It's possible to have some great trades, but it's very difficult to be consistent. This is due to the unpredictability of the market; it cannot be timed with any great degree of certainty. Additionally, institutional traders have more capital to protect them in bear markets(markets in a downward trend), and their trading can trigger retail trader's stop-losses as their buying and selling moves markets up and down very quickly.

There are many factors working against individual investors. Stocks can grow significantly, but they can also decline—or even fall to zero. You should never invest more than you can tolerate losing completely.

In 2020, there was a significant increase in retail traders at the beginning of the Covid-19 pandemic. During this time, many people worked

Financial Understanding

from home or lost their jobs and were looking for new opportunities. Additionally, brokerages were offering low- to no-cost trades to attract more traders and compete with other firms.

Due to fear, uncertainty, and doubt caused by the pandemic, there was a major sell-off.

As these new investors entered the market, they likely saw encouraging results because the market was recovering from this panic. But as the stock market regained much of its losses, people eventually noticed less impressive upward movement. The number of retail traders has since scaled back extensively, further suggesting the difficulty of this investing strategy. It's attractive to follow the markets and look for quick trading opportunities, but ultimately, the odds of success are not in your favor.

Passive Income

An investment strategy that has been very popular among investors is creating passive income. These assets provide regular earnings and require very little effort to maintain. Some stocks provide a dividend, which is paid to investors periodically for holding stock in that company.

Dividends can be paid out as income or reinvested to buy more stock. Researching dividend yielding ETFs and dividend index funds is one way to find investments that are somewhat diversified, allowing more protection than one stock does—which risks failing on its own.

Another passive income strategy is purchasing assets, such as business or rental properties. These investments not only deliver passive income, but their value also appreciates over time, allowing them to be sold at a higher price than purchased for.

In addition to an income stream and appreciation, there are also tax advantages to having these investments.

When considering rental properties, it's important to consider that this requires experience and research to choose the right property in the right market. Looking for properties with upside potential and the ability to find occupants requires knowledge. Purchasing a business also requires knowledge—and can involve significant time upfront to get things moving in the right direction.

Unless you have a degree in business, it's wise to take classes or complete sufficient enough research that will allow you to make knowledgeable decisions. If done well, a successful passive income stream can allow you to work less and give you more time to do what you really enjoy.

Fixed Income Assets

Another lower risk way to protect marginally against inflation is through fixed income assets, such as bonds and short-term CDs. These investments reduce risk, but also yield lower returns.

Stocks and real estate investments normally keep better pace with inflation but have more volatility and risk.

Fixed-income assets work better for short-term goals. For example, if you wanted to buy a house in a few years. This is because goals that are soon approaching can be delayed months or even years if market conditions are poor during that time.

Portfolios

Many successful portfolios blend stocks, real estate, and bonds.

The percentage of each asset class in the portfolio is typically adjusted for how long you plan to invest, and your risk tolerance. It's to your benefit to sit down with a financial advisor to educate yourself about your investment options and to review these with them often. They can help you to strategize for your long- and short-term goals.

Financial Understanding

Some employers offer financial counseling for free, or at a discounted rate. If your employer offers this, it's important you don't overlook it. Investing in securities—whether equities or debt—carries risk. The environment is always changing, so it's good to have ongoing financial counseling for up-to-date information before making decisions.

Continue Learning and Exercising Self-Control

These are just a few concepts that can improve your financial understanding so that you can manage additional funds and work towards your goals. There are many other ways you can learn to make good use of your extra income, as well as ways to grow your savings faster or even build wealth. Exploring the world of finance can improve your understanding further.

Many people prefer to just put it all in savings to reduce their risk, and that works very well for them. Making both a clear budget below your means and a plan designed to reach your goals will let you take control of your finances. It creates a surplus of funds you can use to save or invest.

It will take time, self-control, and patience, because there are so many things that influence you in life. There will be temptations and unexpected things that create many challenges along the way. However, if you focus on what you want to achieve and the benefits of reducing your stress, you will continue making progress.

Passing on Financial Understanding

Putting together a budget, a well-designed plan for future goals, and developing good financial understanding, is important.

It allows you to reach financial freedom.

It's also something you can pass down to your children and other young people in your life. Late adolescents and young college students who are gaining their independence often lack any concept of budgeting—however this simple strategy will give them a great start in life.

It's not typically taught in schools, so you may want to take it upon yourself to teach these strategies to children. You can write out an example budget and show them that every dollar they make below it can be used to build their savings.

You might already show your children how to be smart shoppers by looking for deals before purchasing. This is something they see you doing often, but there is much that happens behind the scenes that most kids don't experience. Things such as budgeting, paying bills, and planning for the future. You can also check in with them later when they begin working to see if they're taking advantage of benefits at work and offer a quick explanation of how these things work.

Passing knowledge to the people you care about is a great way to contribute to their life. If they are resistant, at least it makes it an experience for them. As you know, every experience you have makes you who you are and what you know. What they don't use now, they may in the future.

Conclusion

Getting on top of debt and building savings will give you a wealth of new possibilities. You will start feeling secure and more confident; it removes the stress and anxiety of not knowing whether you can afford even basic things.

Many are experiencing a great deal of hardship due to the Covid-19 pandemic. It hit people financially, emotionally, physically, mentally,

Financial Understanding

and has caused many people to rethink their goals in life. But financial freedom is something everyone can accomplish if you first improve your understanding and make a well-designed plan.

It may take one year to be financially free or five, but it can be done if you're determined. Success means accomplishing your goals no matter what they are.

CHAPTER 5

Ethics

When striving to be a well-rounded individual, you should consider how comprehensive your moral principles are. Over the course of your life, you'll learn what thoughts and behaviors are generally considered right or wrong. You may be taught this, or you may learn through your experiences.

In some instances, your beliefs may be contrary to that of generality, or to different extents; for example, you may not always think public opinion is correct, or you may believe one thought or behavior to be more or less severe than others do.

There is a great degree of variability to people's moral beliefs systems.

Additionally, we make mistakes, your emotions can overpower your judgement, and you may even sometimes choose to proceed with what you know to be wrong due to self-interest or to protect others. These are all examples of when you may forego your own preconceived moral principles.

Furthermore, many of our thoughts arise automatically: You will have to then decide whether these thoughts are acceptable and choose whether to take action. What thoughts should you correct, and to what extent do you regulate your actions? What are your standards? What impact will your conscious acts have on the world and your place in it?

These are personal quandaries which each person faces often. This chapter will delve into various biological drives and ethical concepts for you to examine and consider.

The aim: To arouse interest in further developing your moral system. How much thought will you commit to your own ethical design?

Innate Knowledge, or Experience Only?

It is debated whether we are innately born with some knowledge and morality, or if it all begins building through experience after your mind is formed. This has been deliberated by rationalists and empiricists for some time.

Rationalism claims that you're innate with some knowledge or concepts, and the mind then further deduces things with experience—but experiences can be questionable. Supporters of this argument include philosophers such as René Descartes of France in the early 1600s and go back as far as Plato of Classical Athens.

Rationalists make very good points involving mathematics. They claim that you can deduce things even without the aid of experience. Some see innate knowledge as a trivial part of us, because to what extent would this aid you when you change so much from your experiences?

However, if innate knowledge does exist, it may be the driving factor behind everything you ever believe. This would be very remarkable to understand completely, and many will forever seek answers to this.

Ethics

Alternatively, empiricism states that knowledge is exclusively learned through experience and reflection. Forming something new could be said as plainly as, for example, putting a horn on a horse and calling it a unicorn. It's not intuition, only the combination of experiences.

You experience a horn, you experience a horse, you then put them together to make something new.

Philosopher John Locke supported this theory in the late 1600s. He asserted a "blank slate" theory called "tabula rasa." Locke, and some others before him, believed there is no innate knowledge, and that your knowledge instead comes from perception and experiences occurring after birth.

There are many concepts that provide great support for empiricism. For example, your genes express biological traits which can seem analogous to innate knowledge, but these may just be the mechanisms of structures that were built to their code, and act according to this, adapting as they are able.

Regarding ethics, empiricists believe you can read the emotions of others and determine how they feel based off your own experiences. You believe that they are happy when they smile, or you believe they are sad when they cry because you have had these experiences. Empiricism sees morality as a correct action understood from experience and acquired.

Rationalists argue that just as you can be naturally better than others at something, such as intelligence or the ability to play an instrument, you may rationalize right and wrong differently to others, too. They believe this could suggest that you carry things over from a past life or someplace else.

WELL-ROUNDED

However, it is also possible that your genetic predisposition for a neural network more capable of this skill, combined with your efforts and life experiences, is what makes you capable of a certain skill.

You are also assiduously taught moral principles early in life, and perhaps your ethics come from the constant suppression of your survival instincts due to education and training, as you are questionably more likely to be ethical as a child.

In the eighteenth century, Charles Darwin explained his "theory of evolution by natural selection," which demonstrated how certain genetic traits influence your survival, and ultimately, which characteristics will be passed along through species on account of their endurance.

We can substantiate evolution through natural selection by using observations and experiments to justify why certain traits are good for survival. It may have been that ethically-inclined gene expression was advantageous for survival, that these are therefore moral or knowledgeable tendencies, rather than innate knowledge.

For example, humans who worked together survived greater challenges. And parents who protected their young and taught them to be safe gave them a greater chance of surviving to adulthood and continuing the species.

This is not to state that Charles Darwin himself is a rationalist or empiricist, only that his theory and experiments could support empiricism. Innatism and empiricism aim to uncover the foundations of our knowledge, and further, our motives for morality.

Examining these two theories allows us to question why humans are, and why you should be, ethical. Is this a survival mechanism, something that the fittest passed down genetically as a biological tendency? Or is it something innate, who you were in a previous life, or possibly even given

Ethics

to you by God? Whichever it may be, from when you're born, you're taught societal expectations.

That being said, you may still design your own moral principles above or below given standards.

Early Ethical Teachings

Our moral principles start developing in our youth: You learn from your parents, teachers, and others about what they believe is right and wrong.

But can you really rely entirely on their understanding of things?

You can expect that most of these people have your best interests in mind, after all, they are often responsible if something unpleasant happens to you. And ideally, they teach you important guidelines for basic things in your young life, such as how to be safe and progress towards an encouraging future.

Being taught good values is fortunate, as this will likely help you to avoid consequences in life. But then, at some point, you should recognize that everyone teaches from their perspective, from what they have learned over their lifetime, and what they have decided is right and wrong.

They could very well mislead you, intentionally, or more likely, without even knowing it.

To what extent have they developed their own moral understanding before passing on information they believe to be true? You can choose to use, or disregard, any information given to you—whether learned through experience or reported to you by another.

You may need to compare your information against other reliable sources before you truly believe it. You may also be undecided, with no belief toward something. These are ways you can take control and develop your own morality.

Your Ethical Standard Is Your Choice

In truth, you're not required to have any great extent of ethical standards at all. There are many individuals who don't see ethics as a concern. They choose to be self-serving and even believe this as ideal. There is, in fact, an entire philosophy called "egoism" that suggests just this.

But what would the world look like if everyone thought and acted this way?

Would it be cruel and unsafe? Would we progress as a species? Do these things matter?

You likely feel guilt if your actions hurt someone, or sympathy when you see a person in pain. You also use logic and reasoning to help prevent negative outcomes for other people. Furthermore, you might use your time and resources to help others, even strangers.

Actions such as these likely deny a majorly egotistical world from existing. Moreover, the world is progressing, and people are working together, not just for themselves. So, perhaps our existence could even be dependent on having concern for others.

Keeping an Open Mind

If you are concerned about your ethical footprint, there are many ways to develop yourself. Previously mentioned are some ways you may come upon new information, and further that it is your choice to believe it, to try to further understand it, or to decide it is unreliable.

During this decision-making process, it's important to admit that you may sometimes disregard good teachings, especially from people who have experienced the world longer than you have. Everyone makes mistakes in judgement sometimes, but you can improve by keeping an open mind and allowing yourself to learn.

Ethics

It can be difficult to accept feedback from other people.

You may not like the person, or you may make early judgments about someone and think they have nothing to offer you. But if you don't consider the prospect of new information to some extent, there will be less potential to increase your ethical capacity and to further develop your knowledge in general. You should bear in mind that information will come and go.

If it's your goal to improve, you need to consider each opportunity carefully before it passes.

What We Teach Others

The statements thus far have described some ways you encounter the new information from which you can form your knowledge and beliefs. Appropriately, you should also consider what you yourself communicate to others.

Do you make trustworthy statements using information found through diligence and scrutiny? Do you admit your assertions are to the best of your knowledge? Or do you pressure others to believe things outright? Do you express yourself with good intentions?

Misinformation is spreading universally, and you can contribute to it too. This is of course another argument for you to improve yourself. Many of your beliefs will leave your mind in the form of actions, such as through speaking and moving. These actions will be acknowledged by others, consequently becoming a source of information for them to consider.

They will go through their own process of forming beliefs, and your perceivable actions will have lasting effects because others may use these experiences with you as a source of knowledge going forward. They may also pass this information to others, affecting them as well. If you wish to be more ethical and pass along this knowledge, you must improve yourself to do so.

Developing from Reflection

Moral decision making is often performed impetuously, which may lead to disappointment. Our ethical guard is not always up and ready to react. This is the case with decision-making in general; if you knew the best action to take initially, you would have executed it then.

Although unsettling, this is sometimes the greatest opportunity to improve yourself.

Self-reflection gives you the chance to improve from these types of experiences. Taking some time to think about past events may present opportunities for recovery or improvement for later. If you reflect and determine a better response, you may be able to set things right. Sometimes this means admitting your mistakes, but this reassures that you have met the standards you know yourself capable of.

Reflection also provides you a chance to make improved decisions in the future. Although you may not face this same situation again, you can conceive ideas that improve your way of thinking for the future to help you avoid disappointing circumstances. It's important, though, to discern between thoughts of self-reflection and ones of self-criticism. As discussed in the stress chapter, self-criticism is unnecessary and can be harmful.

Thinking about the problem's cause, a few potential solutions, and then moving forward is more constructive. You cannot expect to know everything about every situation you encounter, but you can learn from each by thinking about them afterwards.

Unethical and Primal Thoughts

Your thoughts can also be unethical. Criticizing, judging, and wanting harm or misfortune for yourself or others are examples of this.

You may judge people for the way they look or for their actions. People are all very different—diversity is what makes the world wonderful; everything is so exceptionally unique. Can you imagine a world where everyone is the same?

It should come as no surprise that people will look and act in a way that you would not. Negative thoughts can be really audacious and impulsive, to what extent can you justify your opinions, even to yourself?

Then again, many of these thoughts can truly be involuntary on your part, you will have many initial and unrefined thoughts that you later become conscious of.

Thoughts like these likely come from your primal brain: The region that controls your most basic needs. This area of the brain is driven for survival and reproduction. Mammals and other animals, especially human beings, have evolved the ability to manage this part of their brain with capacities for ethics and discovery.

Our neocortex is a structure of the brain that, among other functions, allows cognitive skills such as the ability to perceive, reason, and apply logic. It aids decision making and allows you to govern the thoughts and urges that arise from your primal brain. If you *listen* to your thoughts, you can detect whether they have flaws or are morally wrong.

This is an opportunity for you to correct your thoughts before they become beliefs or actions.

Imprudent thoughts can lead to poor choices and consequences for you and others. If uncorrected, they may become habitual, remaining unchecked without reason and consideration. Negative thinking can manifest in behavior and actions without you realizing. But if you desire a higher standard for yourself, you have the faculties to prevent this.

Developing from Assessment

Reflection can help you sort through the past for moral inadequacies, but what about the present moment in time? You can assess your surroundings for things that may influence you to act without regard for ethics. There are many things that can trigger you to produce negative thoughts which may lead to immoral behaviors.

What is your living situation? Do you make time for exercise and relaxation? Are you happy in your profession? Is your life chaotic and unorganized?

Your environment can cause irritability and pressure that can result in apathy for any moral objectives you might have otherwise chosen to carry out. This can also greatly influence your ability to develop further knowledge. Identifying and removing stressful factors and determining what you can learn from your environment will help you be more conscientious in your decision making.

Are there things in your environment causing you a great deal of stress or complication? This can make it very difficult to act morally. If you have too many things going on around you, your life will become busy and hectic. Having too much work and responsibility can lead to quick decision-making that lacks quality effort.

If you don't feel well, it's difficult to be considerate to others and the world around you.

Exercise makes you stronger, energized, and improves your mind. Without it, you lower your ability to do things well. Poor nutrition leads to deficiencies that can cause side effects such as weakness and irritability. Too many calories can slow you down and make you indifferent. Not enough rest and relaxation can cause you to be unfocused and lose patience.

A strong dislike for your career and financial situation can cause you to be miserable and callous. An unorganized life and home can be frustrating and cause you to lose efficiency.

These things are hindrances to your ethical capability. Improving them may not only lead to better ethics, but also improve your life.

Assessing People Close to You

Your environment includes the people in it as well. Other people can have considerable influence over you in many ways. If you have unethical individuals around, they likely have bearing on your knowledge and moral standards.

Anything you experience in your environment is what you have available to learn from. People that historically make careless choices, speak negatively, and lack moral direction can be a source of unethical influence.

Assessing the people around you for these tendencies is necessary to determine how, and if, they affect you as associating with people such as this can make it difficult to act ethically. Even if you're an ethically inclined person, these people are still a source of your information. You can only do your best to provide them with feedback and challenge their opinions that you find to be negative and immoral.

Promisingly, just as negativity can influence ethical people to think poorly, people with good intentions can influence others to be more considerate. If your feedback converts an unethically-minded individual, you may double your efforts in pursuit of good. It can be difficult to change the minds of others, and your opinions may be ignored. But your positive actions can motivate others to develop an encouraging, different perspective.

It's also true that you yourself may sometimes exhibit immoral behaviors without realizing. You can improve this by listening to others and their feedback.

Assessing Other Sources of Influence

Another aspect of your environment that can have great influence on what you learn comes from media and entertainment. News feeds, celebrities, influencers, television, and many other sources of information come with risk and reward. They give you knowledge, moral guidance, and entertainment, but can sometimes be a significant source of misinformation—causing you to attain beliefs based on unfounded claims.

It will benefit you to research questionable statements for evidence-based support before forming new beliefs. This will help you develop a proper belief system.

An interesting concern presents with the way people do research though. They tend to look for the answer that they want to be true. This will be discussed a bit further in the nutrition chapter. Briefly, though, if you search for whether something is ethical, you will likely find something that says it is—there may even be compelling support for it.

The problem can occur if you stop there. Because the same can be true if you ask the same question but replace "ethical" with "unethical." You will likely find very good support for the opposition, too.

Therefore, if you enter a search with a particular outcome in mind, you will find a way to justify it, even if undoubtedly false. It helps to keep an open mind and take into consideration the other side of things. Moreover, you can improve your quality of research by using trusted sources and people educated in your field of interest.

Reasons for Ethics

As mentioned, reflection and assessment are great skills you can use to improve your ethical understanding. You can learn from your mistakes and determine what influences your mindset and learning.

There are also some proactive approaches you can use to improve yourself even further; for example, comparing ethical theories with your current beliefs. This may present you with more information to understand and describe what you believe better.

Before describing some ways to improve your ethical understanding, consider what would motivate you to develop your morality and teach others. What are some ethical challenges in the world, and in your everyday life? With everyone in the world so different from each other, it makes sense that you would need to determine a way to work alongside people.

You have a different understanding of right and wrong from someone else because of who you are and what you've learned. People's actions frequently lead to physical, emotional, and economic harm for others. Societies have instituted laws and policies to regulate people's behavior, which is a great place to start.

Governments and Laws

Laws themselves are not always created ethically. They state what is unpermitted and what privileges people can earn. Laws can be very slow to evolve, even when there are apparent ways to improve how ethical they are.

Sometimes people who are innocent receive punishments without merit, and others to a degree that is not reasonable. Conversely, many people that are truly guilty of crimes escape punishment altogether.

This occurs due to the experience level of legal representation, the jury's experiences and knowledge, the competency of law enforcement to obtain and preserve facts, and many others reasons there may need solutions for. People with poor standards are often given responsibility for decisions that have varying degrees of consequences for other people, which unfortunately, is an issue in any setting.

Outdated laws, and processes for enforcement and judgement, would benefit from reform. If you're responsible for making law and policy, you should expand your ethical understanding and take more risks for good.

Criminals should be required to take ethical classes as a condition of any sentence. This can help fill in some of their gaps in learning to discourage them from further crime.

If you can vote, you can learn more about your governments and communities, and the missions of those who want to fill important positions in society.

Institutions and Policies

Policies and their procedures are also systems that should be responsibly designed.

Just as government officials determine policy within the government, businesses create their own internal policies. Typically, there is a problem that needs to be solved, and then a policy is made to address it. These policies are prepared and managed by those in control, and who have varying degrees of ethical sense.

Ethics

Policy can be made for the good of a company, and that often may not result in ethical consideration. Some businesses are regulated by ethics committees to be compliant with certain standards, and others have their own internal committees, or hire consultants, to assist with this. This is a progressive approach to making change for the better.

However, just as laws are slow to evolve, many companies operate without this oversight and may conduct business at the expense of their employees and clients. Furthermore, it can result in many negative consequences for the environment, which affects all life and the ability for it to continue.

These are some valid concerns for you to look into and improve your ethical understanding.

Reviewing policies, educating company associates, and determining an ethical business model are all important to find and address ethical inadequacies. Employees can also improve their company's standards by identifying poor practices in their business and advocating for change.

Business owners and managers should create a way to receive feedback from employees and customers and then develop an action plan in response to this useful information and any genuine concerns. Many companies already do this and are making change. However, this is slow to come about and therefore consequences continue to occur substantially.

Individual People

You can look at institutions and what they do that contributes to negative outcomes for people and the world, but it is people themselves that design these organizations to carry out the very operations that result in harm.

WELL-ROUNDED

Their conduct, whether in business or in their daily life, carries consequences for others.

This applies to everyone.

Everyone has various poor behaviors that they are either unaware of or simply do not feel concern over. People lie, cheat, steal, and cause mental and physical harm to others.

How can you justify these actions to yourself? Do you even know you do them?

These are more reasons for ethics to be considered and given more attention. By learning more about ethical issues and approaches, you can improve your understanding and beliefs so that your actions contribute to better outcomes.

You're taught basic ideas when you're young, but there are many other things awaiting your discovery. Information that you have not yet even had a chance to consider. Searching for new knowledge about ethics can give you the opportunity to improve your understanding and make conscientious decisions.

Even to this day, many people still discriminate. Not just through thoughts, either, but actions too—it is evident in how people treat others around them. There are people who continue to believe they are somehow superior to others. People discriminate on race, sex, religion, age, and disability. They also discriminate based on how people look, their education level, financial wellbeing, and many other things.

They criticize without knowing a person's situation and what information they have had access to.

Nobody chooses to enter the world differently to someone else. Anyone that cannot conceive that exceptionally distinct life is what makes the world wonderful has lessened their opportunities for development.

Ethics

You do not have to agree with anyone's way of life, but who is anyone to criticize and cut others down for what they believe?

If a person's beliefs cause harm to themselves or others, then they certainly need feedback, more information, and in some cases, disciplinary action. But simple things, such as criticizing someone's way of life or who they are, are simply opinions that cannot be justified.

No one is superior to anyone else; status is only a lifestyle, and authority is a responsibility to uphold. You must decide for yourself what you believe about others.

Sometimes, as mentioned before, you will have primal, impulsive thoughts that are difficult to ignore. But you were also given the ability to manage those thoughts. You can try to improve your government and your businesses, but first and foremost you should improve yourself to learn more and teach others. Offering information and ideas to people versus just blurting out criticism is more constructive.

Although not exhaustive, and undoubtedly not enough justice for the importance of such a matter, these are reasons for why someone may want to consider improving their ethical understanding.

Learning about Ethics

Reflection and assessment are certainly ways to be proactive; this allows you to evaluate your experiences and look to your environment for triggers. This can result in you being more prepared in the future. Yet, you can improve even further by examining ethical teachings to gain greater perspective and ideas to work with.

This chapter presents a couple of different ethical theories, as well as belief systems, to offer you valuable information to improve your ethical understanding. There is no intention here to claim or support that one system is superior to another, or that you should change your beliefs.

WELL-ROUNDED

Many people have already decided their belief system, but you may find more meaning in the beliefs you already possess.

Additionally, this gives you the opportunity to delineate your beliefs better, because you will likely experience an opposing theory. Furthermore, you may encounter new information that adds to your ethical understanding, as it helps you understand why people view things differently.

You may also learn more about how your actions can result in judgements and poor outcomes for people. Others may be inspired by these concepts to form new principles, which they can then use to develop their own belief systems to be more robust and encompassing.

The objective here is provide you perspective and knowledge to improve your ethical awareness. Truly, no one has all the answers to these things, they are simply theories and beliefs that have been debated for centuries. But there are many great sources of information you can learn from regardless. It's especially good to look to those that oppose your beliefs, as this is an opportunity to see differences.

There are many books on ethics, religious texts, and various ethical theories that you can use to improve your understanding. In addition to doctrines, there are stories with challenging scenarios in which people have to make difficult choices. These can help you develop critical thinking, giving you exposure to circumstances where people had to be strong, courageous, true to their beliefs without compromise, make sacrifices, suffer, love, forgive, and more.

These are all very honorable and powerful and inspiring human behaviors.

Although you make many simple ethical considerations every day, occasionally you will face more challenging ones that are more difficult to sort through. Moreover, there are considerations that you don't yet

Ethics

even know exist; you are limited by your knowledge and experiences, which are what improve your perception.

Reading and writing reflections, as mentioned in the mind chapter, are very good for improving your mind. If you write reflections on ethical information, you can improve both your mind and your sense of ethics simultaneously. There are many ethical sources to learn from and you should start wherever you are most intrigued—this will help you stay engaged and learn consistently.

Learning Ethics from Religion

There are many different religions all over the world; there are so many ways people try to find meaning and answers to their existence, such as a creator to show their appreciation or plead their disappointments to. A guardian to look over, protect, and help them with their struggles.

Religion is a powerful practice of faith in God, and it is subjective to everyone that believes in it. There is likely nothing in the world people have made more sacrifices for than this, to such an extent that it has even cost people their lives.

Because of this, there are many courageous stories that show just how far people are willing to go to protect their faith in their God. People will suffer, confess their sins, and sacrifice to help others. Religion not only teaches you how to develop a connection with God, but also teaches you ethics.

Religious texts contain an extensive collection of stories and lessons about right and wrong. Even if you are not a religious person, there are still many ethical principles you can learn through exploring different religions. There are also many corresponding principles from different religions that will help you find consistency across moral perspectives.

For example, many religions, in one way or another, believe in the golden rule: "do unto others as you would have them do unto you."

Although not all traditions state this, the commonality of this concept gives it value.

Religious texts have been criticized for their lack of accurate translation, outdatedness, controlling appearance, and for their conflicting assertions and possibly immoral teachings. But that should not deter you from learning ethics through their teachings—the primary intention of religious teachings is moral integrity.

You will likely develop concerns from any source of material you read from; you do not have to allow yourself to be seduced or convinced by any assertions unless they are truly sensible to you. It will benefit you to see as many perspectives as possible, and then look for consistency across these. As mentioned previously, this will help you form a quality belief system and reach beyond any limited point of view you might have.

The more information you expose yourself to, the more knowledge and understanding you will attain. So much can be understood from religion, and it can embolden you to be stronger and more confident in your beliefs and moral behavior.

Textbooks on Ethics

There are many books on ethics that can give you an introduction to this study. Or, if you have existing experience, you can broaden your understanding through advanced or newly released books. As mentioned before, there is no certainty of what is right or wrong, and because of this, ethics remains a philosophy to be debated, possibly for eternity.

What one person feels and believes is distinctly different from another, and there is really no way to make things right for everyone. Books

Ethics

on ethics therefore aim to develop your understanding so that you can make your best attempt.

They explain different ethical theories and describe the arguments and stories of classical philosophers. Many of them geniuses, or at the very least have contributed work that is still discussed to this day. They have expressed their thoughts with words and writings for you to examine and reflect on their ideas. You can than take these concepts and combine them with your experiences to form new ideas that lead to theories and advancements.

Some of these books contain discussion points in history as well as modern issues in the world today. Unfortunately, philosophy continues to be criticized, which challenges its ability to reach people. There are so many who would benefit from learning about the purpose of philosophy and its contributions.

Philosophy seeks to answer questions such as the nature of knowledge, reality, existence, ethics, and so much more. It is also what has and will continue to be the source of all disciplines and fields ever discovered. People claim that there is no action in philosophy, but it is philosophizing that provokes action.

You need theories and discussion to introduce ideas for experiments and tests, to produce data and evidence, to support facts and find truth. Acting without information and multiple views is a shortsighted approach, vulnerable to mistakes. You don't always have time to discuss things before taking action, but doing so can create a better outcome.

It also inspires change, especially in ethics, because new findings can be presented and warranted. Many people philosophize every day without even realizing it. You may not be given a title for it, but you perform it nevertheless. It helps you to find truth, and to question what you don't yet know and understand.

Ethical Theories

You can behave morally by consciously trying to being kind, caring, and respectful to others. This can be done each day if you learn about people's differences and are mindful of your actions. Improving your knowledge can help you to be more aware.

However, in business, communities, and especially in government, decisions are made that affect many people all at once. Although they can help you with individual decisions, this is where ethical theories really make an impact—politicians need to be transparent in their ethical obligations for decisions that affect the public.

While each theory aims to yield ethical results, there are some strengths and weaknesses to consider.

There are three main theories that are often referred to when many people are involved: Utilitarian ethics, deontological ethics, and virtue ethics.

Utilitarianism is a doctrine that suggests you can achieve the most good if your actions seek to benefit the majority. This is when you should make decisions and policies that result in the greatest amount of good for the greatest amount of people.

On an individual level, you may be less likely to perform an action that would benefit yourself if you knew there was an alternative action that would benefit many people. For example, if someone put up a tree in their yard for aesthetics, but blocked the sun in three other people's yards and caused their plants to die, this person would not be acting for the greater happiness of as many people as possible.

Another example: If the city used public funds to develop the most-used main roads, but it meant rural areas received less funding, a greater amount of people would benefit.

Ethics

In both examples there are people who benefit and people who don't. The minority suffer to benefit the majority. There are many uses for utilitarianism, and it can help you with ethical decision making, but it is not all encompassing, as you can see.

Additionally, how do you measure happiness? And is it more important than things such as your health? Will the decisions you make now for the greater good still apply in the future?

These are some concerns people have pointed out regarding this ethical belief system. Ethics is, and will always be, very complex—you have to realize that there are limitations to any system of ethics and instead see them as guides that funnel decisions towards ethical consideration.

Another ethical theory that will give you a very different perspective is deontology.

This theory states that something is good or bad if it follows an established rule. Some that believe in this system are less strict than others, and for good reason. The objective of this theory is that you have a duty or obligation to follow all rules no matter the result.

This would ideally make decision making very simple: For example, a rule states that stealing is forbidden, and therefore no one will steal. Although very straight forward, deontology in its strictest form is not concerned about the outcome, only the duty. There is no flexibility, even if the results lead to great consequences.

For example, if a counselor learns something about a client that, if revealed, could potentially prevent harm to others, a deontological perspective would typically still prioritize the duty to keep the client's information confidential. Another example: Imagine you come across someone's personal journal containing distressing information. In a deontological approach, you would be morally obligated not to read or share that information, even if doing so could potentially help the person.

WELL-ROUNDED

This can also conflict greatly with utilitarianism as deontology is not concerned with the happiness of the majority; however, minorities would receive better treatment if they somehow were protected by the rule.

It can be comforting to have a very clear way to make decisions. It makes things simple. But life is not simple, and morality benefits from different perspectives and a focus on the desired outcome.

There are different versions of deontology, and some have less stringent beliefs. Despite its weaknesses, this theory has many uses that work well in certain business models where clarity and strict rules for ethical decision making are needed.

Inaction can lead to poor outcomes too; deontology ethics in a well-developed business model can permit immediate action to those who must make immediate decisions.

Virtue ethics is another main belief system, however it is rather ambiguous as it doesn't have the ease and clarity as the above methods. Nevertheless, it's something you can strive for to ensure you act ethically.

Virtue ethics states that it is certain moral traits in a person that makes them ethical. If a person displays acts of loyalty, honesty, kindness, and bravery, they are said to be ethical. It's not concerned with duty and outcome as motivation, it's simply the individual performing moral behaviors.

These can all be great human traits, but they do not always have the outcome of others in mind. For example, an honest person can compromise the safety of others if they are bound by honesty, and as a result, reveal a hidden location that otherwise protects people.

A brave person may enter a risky situation that causes them injury or death.

Ethics

Who will now provide for their children?

A loyal person may look the other way when their friend is causing harm to others and feel content as they themselves continue to be virtuous.

You can achieve many of these traits in the pursuit of virtue while considering yourself moral, but you may want to consider the other two theories as well. Do you have certain duties and obligations to consider? Are there ways you can ensure a good outcome for as many people as possible?

It may then make sense to combine many ethical theories to give you more versatility in your decision making.

Merging Ethical Theories

As you can see, ethical theories limit themselves in many ways. Yet, they can guide us as individuals, and they have many practical uses that work well when we need to make decisions that affect many people all at once, even knowing the outcome will not be right for everyone.

Virtue ethics works well if you want everyone to strive for ethical behaviors, but you could achieve better results if you consider duty and outcomes too.

Utilitarianism is often useful in business and government. Although its weakness is that decisions must be made otherwise all will suffer.

Deontology also works well in business and government in many cases as people need clear ways to operate for efficiency, or they cannot operate very well at all.

However, if you see that a better outcome is accessible, then you should be willing to adapt. Therefore, it's sensible to think of ethical theories as guides that build moral perspectives to give you a more comprehensive ethical understanding.

WELL-ROUNDED

Improving Awareness and Gaining Perspective

Understanding people's differences is also very important for broadening your perspective and improving your ability to be ethical. You can try to be kind and respectful to others. But do you really know how to do this? Do you know how others feel and how your actions affect them? Equally, do you stand up to them, and point out their harmful acts?

Learning about other people requires time and opportunity. You should also determine how far you're willing to go to be ethical for the sake of others and the world.

Are you ever willing to put others' needs before your own? Can you respect them? Should you protect your world?

You will be confronted with many choices, and each situation will present an opportunity to learn and develop your ethics. In doing so, you will contribute more to good, and less to negative, outcomes. Additionally, you will teach others through your conscientious and considerate acts because they will be seen as inspiring.

There are some important things to consider when it comes to other people, animals, and the world that allows you to breathe and carry out your life.

You can gain better perspective through improving your awareness using knowledge, as stated before, but you can also do this by assessing your surroundings for opportunities and looking at the outcomes that follow your actions. This means to escape from your mind and begin gathering information from the world around you.

You learn so much when you increase your awareness and opportunities begin to present themselves. Use your reflection and assessment skills and broaden these to include not only what affects you, but others, too.

Ethics

You will increase your readiness: The ability to see and react quickly. You may be able to spot a chance to hold a door for someone. Or may notice someone's disappointed look and realize your actions caused a problem. There could be a language barrier between you and someone you're speaking to, and you may choose to go to greater lengths to ensure they received your message using a translator app on your phone.

There will be many opportunities to learn and improve your ethics when you increase your awareness. It's not necessary to give away all your possessions and start doing everything for others. In fact, if you give people too much, they may not learn the tools they need for their own survival.

You can respect people and do kind acts for them, but the greatest thing you can do is offer them the knowledge and resources to help themselves. To be most effective, you must always be sure to plan for your family's, and your own, survival before all else.

You cannot help others if you yourself need help.

It is important to address your family's food, shelter, clothes, health care, and resources to get to and from work. You can then help others more effectively and pass on knowledge that will improve their life greatly if they wish to help themselves.

Encountering Immoral Acts

If you desire to achieve a high ethical standard, consider not only your actions, but the actions of others as well. Improving your actions shows that you have developed yourself, but you will often witness people causing harm to others.

What can you do in situations such as these? Will you take it upon yourself to try and help?

If you ignore this, you allow these people to continue their harm unchecked.

There are certain people, because of the way they are, poor upbringing, or other reasons, who do not demonstrate ethical capabilities. Others may grow up learning bad behaviors and be resistant to change. People like this have no ethical sense and will lie, cheat, steal, and harm others.

You can observe these things in your surroundings and take action to stop others from getting hurt. If you are not a professional with experience with these types of people, you can report their behavior before others get hurt.

Sometimes it can be something less physical, such as a coworker that lies to further their own career. It could be to gain advantage over you or someone else. You need to be prepared to defend yourself against these immoral behaviors or determine if you will stand up for others. In these cases, if you see others acting without ethical regard, you can either choose to confront their acts, or overlook their behavior due to fear of conflict or harm.

Moral integrity can carry with it risk and unpleasant situations, but it is the most uncomfortable ones that result in the greatest change.

Improving Awareness in Everyday Situations

Improving your ethical understanding means considering all things involving people, animals, and the world around you. There's a lot of information available about basic things, but it continues to be disregarded. These can be things you do yourself or things you notice others doing.

A small adjustment, a new habit, or a friendly comment to someone can improve the world for everyone.

Ethics

A very common problem affecting the world right now is that many people still choose to leave their homes when they are sick. The spread of germs continues to be a threat because of the choices made by individual people. Viruses must have a host to survive, and if people congregate with others when they're sick, viruses will continue to spread.

Smoking is harmful to health; many smokers know their choice can cause life-threatening diseases for others, and they perform ethical behaviors by smoking in places alone or with other smokers. However, there are some that deny that this is a true risk, or simply do not concern themselves with the fact that it can harm others.

Almost everyone has some form of carbon footprint, some more than others. Learning about how to decrease this as much as possible is a great moral act because it means sacrificing things that would have increased your happiness.

Food consumption has risen to rates that are truly perplexing. In addition to affecting your health, this causes harm to animals because some businesses use unethical practices to keep up with demand.

This also speeds up the rate of resources used and increases the waste that runs into water, air, and the soil.

People recycle, but are you aware of how to do it properly? Recycling companies lose efficiency when it's not done as directed.

These are only a small number of examples in which people can be more ethical, and they each have great effects, such as extending the life of the planet and saving lives. You can gradually find more by learning and improving your awareness and gaining perspective.

Ethical Regard for Animals

We have talked a lot about learning people's differences, but do you also take care and consideration regarding animals?

WELL-ROUNDED

You should consider all the factors involved before adding new responsibilities such as owning a pet. Can you treat them well and give them good living conditions? Can you give them proper amounts of food and hydration? If you neglect their needs, you compromise your ethics.

You don't need to feel bad when you're eating lunch and your German Shepherd is looking at you with depressing eyes, whimpering, and pleading for a bite.

It won't compromise your ethics if you don't cut your sandwich in half and hand it over.

But you want to be sure that your pets' nutrition, living environment, and emotional state are all taken care of. Nearly all animals have nerve endings and experience pain. They also experience emotional damage. There is not sufficient evidence that they experience it the way you and I do because they cannot talk or explain it, but it is more than clear that they become detached, untrusting, and very fearful when treated poorly.

Animals are great companions, and you must treat them well. If you see others neglect their animals, you should explain to them the harm that will result from their actions.

Passing on Ethical Knowledge

When you broaden your understanding of ethics it also allows you to multiply your efforts, because you can pass your knowledge on to others. You can teach your children, friends, neighbors, coworkers, and anyone you see that would benefit from greater understanding.

Spreading good knowledge helps increase awareness on a great scale, as they can pass it along as well. You will likely experience some

Ethics

resistance, but they can use any information they gain for further consideration.

It may be counterproductive to simply call people out for doing something wrong. People don't respond well to this, and they may make worse decisions to try and feel better after their shame. A kind and subtle way will work better.

Bear in mind: Many people just don't know a better way of doing things, just the same as you yourself continue to learn better ways too. Asking questions sometimes gets a message across to people with less risk of offending them.

For example, "Did you know that putting plastic in a glass bin will cause difficulties for the recycling companies?" Or "Did you know that using a water bottle filled with water from home reduces plastic waste, is healthier, and saves money all at once?"

There will be many people that simply do not care, and they may argue and criticize unnecessarily. But if even one person changes their habits after receiving your information, you will be going beyond what you can do on your own.

Ethics Versus Happiness

Is your happiness more important than ethical issues?

You can certainly achieve happiness and be ethical, but there will be times when you need to choose between them. You may be motivated to be ethical to meet your standards, due to a fear of consequences, or a sense of duty.

But there are times when you may compromise your ethics for happiness.

You may even find ways to justify it to yourself.

This can become habitual, and you may not even know. But if you still want to have higher standards, there are many ways you can improve. It can help to be forward thinking about it. Erik Erikson, a German developmental psychologist, stated his theory of human development in eight stages.

In the final stage of development, "Integrity versus Despair," he says that after about age sixty-five up until you pass, you may believe one of these two things about yourself. If you believe yourself to have "Integrity," you likely feel content and well-achieved when looking back on your life. If you have too many regrets, you may feel disappointment, thus, "Despair."

What are you setting yourself up to feel when that day comes? Are you currently at this stage in life and looking for ways to be kind, respectful, and to pass on your knowledge and wisdom to others? Ethics may not only be important for how you feel at the end of your life. These ethics may be how we have survived as a species thus far; they demonstrate powerful, compassionate human attributes, and allow people to work together.

Conclusion

You help others that struggle, and they help you. Sometimes you just don't know how your actions affect others, therefore, increasing your knowledge and understanding can help with this.

You can improve your perspective by learning, assessing your environment, and reflecting on your experiences. The ideas described in this book are minimal in comparison to what you can learn. Additionally, you can combine it with everything else you've experienced, and continue to into the future.

Ethics

If you aspire to develop your ethical understanding, you can establish your own standards and strive to achieve them. It will not always be easy, and your happiness may often be sacrificed. But it's your choice—you have control over your own ethical design.

PART II

Health

Having a healthy mind increases your ability to manage all other aspects of your life. It can improve your decision-making skills when handling relationships, finances, stress, and integrity.

It can also lead to better overall health and wellbeing—but there is much more to your health than just your mind.

Addressing your overall heath is just as important because it can avert and manage many of the causes of your problems. Your health affects things such as mood, energy, focus, and your ability to do things. Poor health can also cause setbacks, missed opportunities, and extensive financial troubles.

You may be experiencing some of these problems currently, so by improving your health, you will feel better and boost your desire to do things.

People often overlook their health until they develop new or bigger problems. This can make it more difficult to improve or manage them. By taking control of your current health issues and learning to prevent others, you can enjoy a better quality of life.

WELL-ROUNDED

This section discusses simple ways to develop an understanding of your health, and aspects of it that are often neglected, misunderstood, and necessitate greater awareness. A recurring notion in this book is that you need to experience things; you must gain exposure to achieve understanding and appreciation.

Experience increases your knowledge so you handle things more effectively.

Health information always seems to be changing, and this can be very frustrating. What's said to be healthy one day is harmful the next. But change is inevitable as knowledge continuously evolves alongside better understanding. It is simply information being corrected and updated.

For this reason, doctors, lawyers, and other professionals must undergo continuous education as new information emerges. It can be disappointing when things come out prematurely, but research done correctly has its benefits. It benefits all disciplines to improve and make further information available to ensure the best decisions possible.

If you expand your perspective on your health, you can make adjustments that prevent and manage your health issues better. You can also improve your strength, energy, and how you feel, making life more enjoyable.

CHAPTER 6

Understanding Health

Many people experience low energy, trouble sleeping, irritability, and countless other problems that make it difficult to work and enjoy everyday things. There are also problems that develop without you noticing, as they don't present themselves clearly to you.

These problems can become more serious health issues if they go on undetected.

Additionally, we make everyday choices that put us at risk of chronic conditions such as increased blood pressure, cholesterol, and sugar levels. These can result in diseases such as diabetes and heart disease among others. Health problems are expensive to manage and can cause great harm to your body and ability to do things.

Furthermore, disregarding your health can speed up your aging. You've probably noticed a person who looks like they're in their twenties, only to find out they're indeed in their forties. Sometimes, this is down to genetics—but often that person makes lifestyle choices that slows their aging as opposed to others that are speeding it up. That person looks younger, healthier, and more energetic.

Understanding and addressing your health can help you feel significantly better while identifying serious health concerns. You can learn which changes will decrease risk factors for developing diseases and how to manage or improve ones that have already begun.

This will result in better health and will make you more active and better prepared for life's challenges and pursuits. Many people believe that improving their health will just allow them to live longer. Although this is true, you also live *healthier* for longer.

Living healthier for longer allows you to be more capable of doing everyday things. You will have more energy and muscle, strong bones, and a capable mind. Taking control of your health will greatly improve how you feel and perform.

Reasons for Inadequate Health Knowledge

There are many reasons why you might not have an adequate perspective of your health needs. When you're young, you don't typically build a good understanding of your health as your parents make most of these decisions for you.

The information that does reach you is often disregarded because you feel fine most of the time. Additionally, you might develop a negative association with healthcare because of injections and testing. You might have found a doctor's office uncomfortable and wished to avoid it.

This creates early attitudes of avoidance and a limited understanding that healthcare is there only for serious complications. The useful information that *is* received about healthcare begins to fade over time, and by the time you're an adult, you lack a good understanding of important health services.

Understanding Health

During this time, your health goes unmonitored, and you lack quality information about stress, proper nutrition, and other important health considerations. Additionally, some of the information people do obtain can be false. This puts you at greater risk of feeling miserable and of developing health problems.

Conversely, if you had a health condition growing up, you might have gained a very good understanding of your health through frequent doctors' visits. You might have a disease such as type-1 diabetes. In this case, you learn to understand your disease, and how to manage it yourself to some extent.

Women may also have more frequent experience with healthcare for reasons such as birth control; in this case, you often learn to manage these things and be more proactive about your health early in life.

Additionally, if you're a young athlete, you would gain more experience with your health as you'd need additional physicals, and you would be given extensive information about how to monitor and maintain your health and fitness.

This is how some young people come to have a better understanding of important health decisions, how to identify problems better, and stay connected to their health throughout their life. If you have a good grasp on your own health, it can be fortunate for the people around you; you may be able to notice changes in others' health that they don't pick up on themselves and encourage them to seek healthcare right away.

This can sometimes help get people more involved in their health, and learn about risk factors, healthier behaviors, and how to prevent serious health consequences.

WELL-ROUNDED

Getting Your Health Status and Learning Your Risk Factors

The first step in taking control of your health is establishing a primary care provider and having a physical exam completed. This way, you can get an immediate health status and learn about your risk factors.

At the time of writing this book, most health insurance plans pay for an annual physical exam at no cost to you because it's a preventative service. This is a great way to make use of what you're already paying for. Budgeting for health insurance is an important and conscientious decision. If you don't have access to health insurance, there are many services through the state and federal government that may make healthcare more accessible to you.

Some doctor's offices also have discounts for the uninsured.

A physical exam gives you the opportunity to get completely assessed. Doctors will examine you, run tests, and give you your health status. They also obtain a family history, a list of current problems, prior surgeries, prior diagnoses, immunization history, and track and document all your health problems, allowing them to understand your needs and detect important changes.

This records your health over your lifetime, making it much easier to manage.

During their assessment, the doctor can find any concerning health problems and recommend treatment. They can also refer you to other specialists, registered dieticians, therapists, or others that have extensive training and experience treating people with similar problems that you might have.

They will also explain what risks you have and how you can make better health decisions. It's important to find a doctor you feel comfortable with as they need to know all your health-related issues in order to help. You will feel more open with someone who is pleasant, capable, and shows concern for you.

Not everything will show up in tests and exams, so you need to explain what's going on in your head and with your body honestly. They have limited time, so they cannot help you decide which color paint you should use in your living room, but with real health concerns such as feeling down, a lack of desire to do things, anxiety, pain, or something about your body that doesn't seem right. The more they know, the better they can help you.

If something new arises in between visits, at the very least, contacting the nurse will help you determine whether you need to be seen. You might, like many, have developed a negative mindset towards healthcare. However, when you get answers as to why you don't feel well, receive treatment or information to help you get better, and learn ways to prevent bigger problems, you can feel reassured and improve your health.

Protecting Your Health

Undergoing physical exams and seeing your doctor when you have a concern are great ways to stay on top of your health. Both taking your medicine as directed and scheduling maintenance visits will help manage your health problems so you can be at your best.

In addition to this, there are many things you can do to increase your chances of good health when you see your physician. Understanding more ways to improve your health, and what things might be harming it, will give you more energy, slow down aging, and reduce your chances of developing new health problems. Many things discussed in the first chapter about keeping your brain healthy are important for your body, too.

It's very important to use safety methods to prevent injury and to understand which chemicals you are using at home and work that are harmful to your body. These are, in fact, major reasons for many hospital visits each year.

Injuries can occur in so many ways and result in broken bones, cuts on the skin that can become infected, damaged joints, and more. Ingestion and absorption of chemicals through the skin and eyes is also common and can be very toxic. Using safety equipment such as gloves will save you time, money, suffering, and so much more.

Avoiding smoking, drugs, and alcohol was also mentioned in the mind chapter. There are many organs in the body other than the brain that can be harmed by these. They can also cause injury, reduced energy, lost time, faster aging, and less control over your finances and responsibilities. Drugs and alcohol can damage your relationships and make it very difficult to progress in life.

Interestingly, people that choose to stop these addictions tend to have amazing lives after. It's as if they needed to replace their addiction with something to keep their minds from it. As a result, many people become very connected to things such as health and fitness.

Some become vegans and educate themselves about healthy food choices. Others have incredible fitness achievements and do more outdoor activities. Many make extensive improvements in their home and work life and become very successful.

You often don't know how much time and energy you really have until you change things that are impeding your ability.

Improving Your Health

There are many things you can do to improve your health so you can perform at your best. An example of this is managing your weight; this is something that can be very difficult for people.

Many body builders find it just as difficult to increases their muscle mass. It's as if your body is stubborn to change and just wants what's easiest. But just as discussed in the mind chapter, difficulty is what improves you. You learn from challenges, and your body adapts resultingly. There are people constantly changing their mindset and finding ways to achieve what can seem like impossible goals. Improving your weight will give you better health, energy, confidence, happiness, and so much more.

The fitness section of this book describes some additional ways you can become motivated and determined to reach your health goals.

Nutrition Factors

Your environment and available options often set you up for failure. People are known to choose taste, texture, and flavor over health.

Companies sacrifice nutrition content for these things because they know meeting these desires will sell their product. Packages and labeling can be manipulative and are often designed by psychologists who know your weaknesses.

Unhealthy foods are typically the easiest to make and can save you time and energy. Proper nutrition can also be very difficult to understand as many sources tell you one thing and others contradict it.

This is all unfortunate as your diet is the most important part of your health. You can lower your risk of disease and maintain a healthy weight with your diet alone. However, you can achieve better weight management results and greater health if you combine this with exercise.

If you want to improve your health, proper nutrition is a primary factor—therefore, this will be discussed in more depth in the next chapter.

Weight Management

Exercise goes hand in hand with nutrition. You need this to burn the excess calories you have consumed. There are other factors, but diet and exercise are the way to success for most people. Exercise is incredibly important to your health in many ways. The next section of this book will discuss fitness in greater detail, as regular exercise will maintain your health, improving fitness provides greater rewards such as improved performance, greater health, flexibility, and it can make you look and feel younger.

Exercise is essential for your health and can help you control your weight much faster. To achieve weight loss, you need to burn more calories than you consume. Although this easier said than done, it's just math; the energy must come from somewhere when you are exercising.

You will need to burn through your reserves, and then you will start breaking down body fat for more energy. The reserves are stored as glycogen in your liver and muscle cells from your recent meals. This energy is just easier for the body to access and break down, so it burns through this first. After that, your body breaks down fat for energy, and the by-products leave the body as carbon dioxide and water, effectively reducing your weight.

Since there is a lot of energy in fat, it can take time and commitment to see the results you want. Additionally, there are many foods we consume that have a surprising number of calories, so it's important to scrutinize your intake so that you get the expected results from exercise.

Bear in mind there is never a temporary fix to weight management. It will need to be maintained for a lifetime. Therefore, making diet and exercise something you enjoy will make it much easier. Many of the people that you see managing great health and fitness simply love doing it.

Exercising for Complete Bodily Health

Exercise is important for weight loss, but there are many other areas of your health to consider too. Having a complete exercise plan will help you to improve all areas of your body.

Cardio is great for your heart and brain and builds muscle strength in many areas of the body. Adding weight training can help you build muscle and strengthen your bones. Walking is also very important for bone strength—and can be great for the mind.

Stretching and properly warming up are essential to prepare your joints and prevent injury. If workouts are incomplete, you will miss some of these important benefits. Your exercise requirements will also be unique to you, many factors such as age, disability, and health conditions will influence them. You need to perform the ones that are right for you.

If you're having trouble with weight management and are unsure which exercises are right for you, you can get the assistance of personal trainers, registered dieticians, and doctors who have many effective solutions for each body type and health status.

If you're having trouble with motivation, you will need to try and shift your mindset. One thing that really helps with this is to increase your base activity level. Through this, you will likely start enjoying physical activity and wish to achieve more strength and energy to go further.

Sometimes, you probably think about going on a walk, or someone might ask you to go but you really don't feel up for it. People are often amazed that when they do get up and start walking—the prior feeling of apathy fades away quickly, and you start really enjoying it.

Sometimes, all it takes is just getting started with an activity to change your mindset around doing it.

Hydration

Proper diet and exercise will do amazing things for your mind and body. They allow you to control many of your risk factors for disease, and improve how you think and feel. At the same time, it's important to keep hydrated. You might be making many of the right choices, but still feel poorly. If this the case, drinking water might help.

Proper hydration is very important to how you feel and perform. People can get into a habit of consuming lots of high-sugar drinks, which is dehydrating and leads to many health problems such as weight gain, diabetes, and inflammation. Replacing these drinks with water not only reduces your calorie intake but also saves your teeth from harm, and lowers your risk of disease.

Since consuming high-sugar drinks can be habitual, it can be difficult to stop drinking them—especially if you enjoy them. The best way to deter these habits is to reduce your access to them. Remove them from your home and office and other places they're stored. Carrying a bottle of water will give you access to a healthy choice, build a good habit, and save money.

It's also important to drink water when you first wake up in the morning. It's difficult to stay hydrated when you're asleep.

Everyone's hydration needs will be different, and you will need to drink more when you increase physical activity. When you're not feeling well, try drinking a glass of water or two. You might be shocked by how quickly it improves how you feel.

Our First Line of Defense

Your skin is very important for maintaining your health, but it's frequently neglected. Your skin is your largest organ and it protects you from harmful things in your environment. It has some shock absorption against trauma but breaks in the skin and damage to lower tissues can still occur.

It protects against bacteria and is one of your first lines of defense against chemicals, microorganisms, allergens, and the sun. It's important to eliminate the handling of any chemicals without proper protection because the skin can still absorb them. It will also benefit you to scrutinize your skin products. You may believe them to be safe, but some will dry out your skin and may contain unsafe chemicals.

Having multiple sexual partners without protection and without knowing their prior history can also expose you to both short- and long-term diseases. Your hands touch so many things such as door handles, shopping carts, and handrails, and the moisture on your skin makes it very easy to pick up microorganisms and bring them with you.

In most cases, these things are not visible as they are extremely small. Microorganisms can then enter the body through the eyes, mouth, nose, and open cuts and wounds. Just as others leave germs for you to pick up, you can leave them behind in the same way, so leaving home when you're sick can harm others.

All breaks in the skin should be covered until healed, unless otherwise directed by a physician, and you should wash your hands often to reduce your chances of infection. This information is widely available, and you probably hear it often, but skin infections, chemical exposure,

STDs, and illness are still top reasons for healthcare visits.

This can cause loss of time, expenses, and make you feel miserable. However, with proper health practices, you can greatly reduce your risk of sickness and infection.

External Aging

Considering that skin cells on the outside of your body are all dead, your skin is incredibly beautiful. So many variations in color and uniqueness in every individual. It contributes greatly to your identity. People tattoo and pierce it and find many ways to express themselves with their skin.

Taking care of your skin will allow you to maintain its beauty for as long as possible.

Skin is exposed to the elements, so there are many factors that cause it to age quickly. You can also develop skin disorders, such as eczema, psoriasis, and acne, though these are often out of your control. These disorders need a board-certified dermatologist as early as possible to reduce the accumulation of harm to your skin. However, many things are preventable, and you have control over them.

As well as wounds and injuries, the accumulation of sun damage can cause major concerns. Although sun exposure allows you to create much-needed vitamin D, it also has damaging ultraviolet radiation. Being outdoors has so many benefits for your mind and body, but prolonged sun exposure can speed up the aging of your skin.

Dermatologists can do full skin exams to find abnormal moles, skin cancers, and look for other abnormalities. Older patients frequently have extensive blemishes all over their skin, which is not immediately apparent until they compare the sun exposed areas, such as the arms and back, to the nonexposed areas such as the upper thighs and buttocks.

Areas that get infrequent sun exposure may be completely clear of any blemishes except for perhaps some moles you've had since you were young. The DNA damage from the sun is accumulative over your lifetime, so it can really add up. In addition to age spots, speeding up the aging of your skin will reduce its strength and elasticity, causing it to become thin and break easily.

You can develop skin cancers anywhere, so you should identify and have examined anything that is progressively changing, as well as any bumps or masses below the skin. Hot showers dry out your skin, so room temperature or cold showers are a healthier choice. Quitting smoking will also stop the harmful narrowing of blood vessels so your skin receives more oxygen and nutrients.

In contrast, exercise dilates blood vessels and brings a great supply of oxygen and nutrients to the skin as well as removing waste. Exercise and fitness training can also tighten the skin and make it healthier and better looking. It can be difficult to remember to take care of your skin, so building good habits such as carrying sunscreen will help you stay prepared.

Inhalation

As mentioned, you can be exposed to chemicals and germs through skin-contact. They can also gain entry through your nose and mouth. You are very often inhaling harmful things into your lungs. Chemicals are toxic to you, yet people use them every day. Chemical sprays are sometimes replaced with wipes; however, you can inhale chemicals in this way, too.

Finding natural substitutes is better for your health and is very effective for cleaning. Baking soda, hot water, and vinegar all work very well for cleaning and are less harmful in proper amounts. Alcohol and hydrogen peroxide are natural alternatives but can also cause irritation to the lungs. Lemon can be added for a fresh smell and even greater disinfection.

These options can help you greatly reduce the amount of toxins you inhale daily. If you live in a major city, you are likely still inhaling carbon monoxide and many other pollutants that are in the air. Therefore, it's ideal to reduce as much chemical exposure as you can.

The accumulation of damage to your lungs can reduce your performance and lead to disease. Just as germs can infect you through skin contact, so too can you inhale them into your lungs. Even with great hand hygiene, you can still get sick if you're around others who are coughing and sneezing as you will inhale microscopic water droplets in the air. This is why it's important to stay home when you're sick and avoid others that are ill.

Healthy Teeth and Gums

Sugar is one of the most detrimental things to your body, yet, it is still widely used in many of the foods and drinks we consume. It can cause harm to your organs, blood vessels, and nerves.

It can also cause extensive damage to your teeth. When sugar enters the mouth, it sits on your teeth and the bacteria there convert it to acid, which can start breaking down the enamel. It can take minutes for the sugar to leave your teeth and having another sugary drink or snack starts the process all over again. Diet sodas and many other carbonated drinks are also acidic, so they are not healthy substitutes.

Understanding Health

You can also harm your teeth through smoking, poor dental hygiene, biting things that are hard, and even brushing too aggressively. Protecting your teeth will help them last longer and prevent you from the discomfort and financial challenges that often result from lack of care.

Dental hygiene is also important to prevent gum disease.

If you've ever met someone in their twenties or thirties, or even younger, who has lost some teeth, it's quite possible they lost them due to gum disease. Good dental hygiene can prevent this from happening. And although dental visits can be unpleasant, you can sustain great teeth for longer and prevent more uncomfortable visits by seeing your dentist as often as they recommend.

Posture

Another thing that happens as you age is your posture declines, literally. It can be difficult to catch this happening so you will benefit greatly by being aware of it and building good habits as soon as possible.

Poor posture can lead to difficulty breathing because you are restricting the expansion of your lungs. It can cause back and neck pain because of the strain that it causes them. This can also lead to headaches because of the pressure it puts on the muscles in the shoulders and neck. It can lead to problems with sleep because of pain and difficulty relaxing. Additionally, it can also put pressure on joints in the spine, which can weaken them.

Fortunately, you can improve your posture—and if you experience any of these symptoms, they may improve as well. Using correct posture and adding things to your routine such as stretching, yoga, and muscle strengthening can all help.

Since doctor's offices record height so often, they keep all this data available for you. It's not uncommon for an older person in their sixties or seventies to find their height has increased after regular stretching or yoga sessions. This can be very encouraging.

It does take time and commitment to improve posture, and it can begin to decline again if you return to poor habits. It's also expected you will experience some strain and pain while building up the muscles to correct your posture, so you should use the correct methods gradually so you don't injure yourself. Improving your posture has great benefits for your health, comfort, and appearance.

Slowing Normal Decline

It gets much harder to maintain your body's health as you age. Diet becomes even more important for preventing and managing diseases.

Your skin and immune system gets weaker, increasing your chances of sun damage, infection, and slower healing.

Muscles weaken, making it difficult to maintain strength.

Bones can weaken, making them susceptible to fractures. Falls happen to be a leading cause of death for elderly patients, so maintaining muscle and bone strength is essential.

Being as active as possible is very important. This is the "use it or lose it" concept that is so important to your health. Your bones, muscles, and brain all benefit from use and will decline without it. Disability can occur at any point in life, though the chances of it increase as you get older. This makes maintaining your health much more difficult.

Disabilities require creative strategies to make exercise possible and to avoid further harm. Although discouraging, there are many options to help you work around your disease or disability if you are affected by such, and you will feel much better and capable because of it.

If you encounter the loss of any ability, it's important to learn how you can continue as many activities as possible. Your body can be very content without exercise, so you will have to take control to improve. Adjusting for challenges to improve your health will keep you performing as optimally as possible.

Organization

Another recurring topic in this book is organization. Having all the aspects of your life well organized makes everything easier. Maintaining a well-cleaned home and yard can improve your health, reduce stress, and prevent injury.

Having lists that you can refer to for healthy meal ideas can make it easier to avoid grabbing something quick that is either unhealthy or lacking nutrition. A list that you can add new goals to will remind you to look for opportunities.

A well-developed schedule that includes exercise, medication, and relaxation will also make your goals easier to achieve. Updating your lists and reminders allows you to continuously improve them. If you fall off your schedule, continue with it as soon as possible or make a new one. It's surprising how much extra time you'll have when you're well organized.

Advocating for Health Improvements

Yet again, passing on good knowledge helps others. If your health is improving, share your experience. Let people know that eating right and exercise is working well for you, and they will likely see these changes readily. You can encourage them to investigate their options to see what benefits they can achieve.

It's likely they just haven't received the right information or lack motivation to change. It can be inspiring to see someone they know looking healthier, stronger, and more energetic. They may be motivated to improve because they can see that it's possible. It's important, though, to avoid any criticism because this will likely have the opposite effect.

You won't motivate anyone by attacking their health, appearance, or activity level. They can feel pressured, and it can make them push away from you. Letting them know you're feeling great after taking your health seriously—and that you believe other people can find ways to do it too—is a great way to be considerate and pass on the information.

You can also help your children become better connected to their health and fitness. Children love to hear that they are healthy, and when they are not, they become very involved and ask many questions about what they can do to improve. Helping them to build a good relationship with doctors and finding activities they like will help them get more experience and information about their health.

Conclusion

Health can be a challenging topic for many. This is because, to achieve good health, it involves reducing or giving up many things you really enjoy. It can also require many activities and learning about things that your body doesn't always feel like doing. But these sacrifices and changes will be rewarded with great benefits.

They can also reduce limitations, suffering, and financial hardships later in life. To have good health you need to be forward thinking. Many things that are harmful to you are risk factors that are *quietly* progressing and adding up until they eventually result in disease or limitation.

Understanding Health

This is because your body is very strong and is working hard to keep you well. It continues to fight for you, but it needs your help if you wish to be healthy and perform well.

CHAPTER 7

Understanding Nutrition

Many health problems are due to your diet. Therefore, you can reduce your risk through healthier food choices. Unfortunately, only a small percentage of available foods are healthy. You can certainly get energy from most foods, but many cause health problems due to inadequate nutrition, additives, and high caloric content.

As mentioned before, it's advantageous for companies to sell things you'll buy, even if they are not healthy for you. Therefore, you may not want to rely on businesses to provide healthy choices. Instead, you can determine which foods are better to consume and adjust your selections over time.

Foods with extensive amounts sugar, other additives, harmful fats, and pesticides can increase your chances of disease. Consuming more calories than you need for energy can also be harmful to your health as it can increase weight. Your body naturally stores excess calories because it is unsure when your next meal will be. Consequently, you'll need to watch the number of calories you consume and look for changes in your weight, too.

WELL-ROUNDED

There is a long list of health consequences that result from excess weight, and it can also make it difficult to be more active. People that are not overweight can have similar health concerns and they require proper diets and exercise to be healthy, too. Micronutrients such as vitamins and mineral are also very important as deficiencies can cause low energy and other uncomfortable symptoms. Over-supplementation of vitamins and minerals can lead to toxicity.

All these factors are important for your health and how you feel. Nutrition can be difficult to get right, and it isn't made easy for you to achieve. However, many people have improved their understanding of it and maintain their health very well. A healthy diet can set you up to be more energized and feel great each day. This chapter will explain important areas of nutrition and easier methods to improve yours.

Monitoring Your Health Status

As mentioned in the last chapter, determining your health status is always the first step. Having a physical exam will let you detect health conditions, such as high blood pressure and cholesterol, so they can be managed. You can also determine whether you have developed, or are at risk for, heart disease, diabetes, or other diseases.

These health problems commonly result from a combination of poor diet and your genetics. As they can be due to your genetics, people who are extremely health conscious with food choices and exercise can still develop disease. Physicals are also an important time to check for nutrient deficiencies to determine whether you need to change your diet, or supplement it, to achieve the proper amounts. Your doctor can recommend treatments and refer you to a registered dietician to help you learn the most up-to-date nutrition and supplementation practices.

Understanding Nutrition

You can also use a Body Mass Index (BMI) to determine where your weight should relatively be. This is a quick tool you can use to determine which weight range to aim for. There are better methods for determining health, as this does not measure body fat, so it's important to ask your doctors whether this tool will work for you. Then, you only need to log your height and weight into a BMI calculator and determine what you need to gain or lose to reach the indicated healthier range.

Your doctor can also provide your BMI with your health status report, which is just the documentation from the exam.

Understanding and Managing Calorie Intake

Reaching and maintaining a healthy weight is a great way to start improving your health.

You can get started by recording your calorie consumption to determine the amount you typically consume each day. A couple weeks of data can really put things into perspective. If you're consuming extensive amounts of calories, you may want to work on ways to curb the desire to eat and change which foods you're consuming. Foods containing fructose, simple sugars, and food additives can trick you into believing you haven't consumed enough, meaning you'll eat more.

Learning which foods have this potential will help you avoid them.

Drinking water before eating is a great way to fill your stomach some before a meal. Replacing high calorie foods with low calories foods is also very helpful. What you have access to is what you eat, so this chapter will explain simple ways to improve the healthy options available to you.

You can begin by making healthy food lists and replacing poor food items with better ones: Start a food list for breakfast, lunch, dinner, snacks, and drinks. Once this list has evolved over days, weeks, and months, you can create a list of recipes for each category. This will make decision-making very easy; you will only have these items in your home, so you choose from these lists what you wish to eat.

This evolves over time, but it's always ready, saving you time and making it less likely you'll grab something that hasn't been vetted. Once you have investigated foods and determined they are healthy, you can add them to your list. If you learn new information that a food on your list is unhealthy, or you simply don't like it, you can remove it.

It's important to change your diet slowly—trying to change everything at once makes it difficult to manage, and may lead to frustration and deterrence from your goals. Additionally, it's important to consume meals that contain essential macro and micronutrients.

The next part of this chapter will explain some healthy and unhealthy food choices, and then will go on to discuss great strategies for implementation.

Pesticides

When switching to healthier foods you should anticipate there will likely be a cost difference—especially in the beginning when you're trying to determine healthier foods. Some may spoil before you get to use them because you're trying to learn new recipes and the quantities to have on hand, and healthier foods generally cost more anyways.

So, this chapter will later explain ways to improve efficiency.

It can also help to use the money management strategies from the financial understanding chapter. You can do this by adjusting your budget to accommodate for increased food costs. The immediate increased costs will likely reduce over time as you learn better strategies and find places that have healthier foods at lower costs. You can then buy more organically-sourced foods.

Understanding Nutrition

Foods made with pesticides are harmful to your body. There are general guidelines for harmful chemical quantities and people know to wash their fruits and vegetables before preparing a meal. However, it's still a risk to you anytime you introduce harmful chemicals into your body.

It's unwise to trust that companies are not capable of error and use products that can kill bugs but won't harm you in any way.

People consume varying levels of these harmful chemicals, so you might build up great amounts of them in your body. You're not fully aware of the short- and long-term harm this can do to you: In large amounts, some of these chemicals can cause kidney and liver damage, as well as DNA damage, which can lead to organ failure and cancers. Foods sprayed with chemicals may, or may not, be healthy to eat, but you can reduce your risk if you shift to organic foods that are responsibly produced.

Processed Foods

Whole foods are a much healthier option as processed ones lose nutrients during processing and may contain additives. Processing food at home and cooking everything from scratch is a better option because you know everything in it.

Cooking and consuming the food shortly after processing also has more nutritional value then allowing it to sit for hours and days. Industrial food processing requires companies to decide how they will keep foods looking desirable and from spoiling before they reach the consumer.

Perishable and non-perishable foods can contain these preservatives and other additives, such as added sugar, sodium, unhealthy fats, and artificial colors and flavors.

These practices result in foods with minimal nutritional value. They can cause blood sugar spikes that are known to cause insulin resistance. Excessive sodium products can lead to high blood pressure, which can cause heart disease. Some increase your cholesterol. Eating a lot of processed food increases your risks of sickness and disease greatly. Transitioning to whole foods is a healthier alternative.

Simple Sugars

As discussed previously, reducing simple carbohydrates as much as possible is a healthier choice as they can be harmful to you. Although you can get energy from these sources, they lack essential nutrients and fiber.

Excessively and frequently eating simple sugar foods can lead to metabolic syndromes which cause weight gain and increase risks for health conditions and diseases. Simple sugars such as glucose can be broken down easily and used for energy. Fructose, however, is a sugar that is much more threatening to your health.

Fructose will not stimulate the hormones that tell you you're full, so it's more likely you'll consume more calories. Also, this sugar can only be broken down by the liver, and a large amount will be stored as fat. This can lead to a buildup of fat in the liver, which can result in a health condition called "fatty liver."

You can also get this condition through excessive alcohol consumption.

Fatty liver can cause inflammation and scarring of the liver, which can decrease its performance and may lead to more serious problems such as liver failure and cancer.

Fructose can also increase your bad cholesterol levels, thereby increasing your risk of heart disease. It is the sweetest of sugars and, consequently, very desirable. Therefore, many companies and people add them to foods. This can result in consuming more of this very unhealthy sugar. Complex carbohydrate foods contain longer lasting sugars and fiber which are less likely to spike your blood sugar, and also contain other nutrients such as vitamins and minerals.

Choosing complex carbohydrates over simple ones can keep you feeling full for longer and can improve your health, weight, and energy.

Carbohydrates

Carbohydrates can be difficult to add to your diet healthily, but whole foods are a great start.

Looking for high fiber foods is a good choice as they can benefit you in many ways. Fiber can slow down digestion and keep harmful sugars and cholesterol from being absorbed. This reduces your chance of blood sugar spikes and high cholesterol levels. They are also more filling, so you'll eat less and stay satisfied for longer which can help you improve and maintain a healthy weight.

It can also keep your bowels healthy, and help avoid constipation and diarrhea, helping you to maintain feeling well. You can also look for carbohydrate foods with a low glycemic index. These foods are less likely to spike your blood sugar levels.

High glycemic foods include white rice, white bread, and potatoes. Low glycemic, healthier carbohydrate foods, include starchy vegetables, such as sweet potatoes and yams, and non-starchy vegetables such as broccoli and cabbage. These foods have a wide range of nutrients and are a healthier source of carbohydrates.

Protein

Protein was described in the first chapter to be important for brain health, but it's also necessary for building and repairing essentially all tissues in the body. It's used in many biological processes and is important for how you carry oxygen to all your living cells.

Avoiding red meats or buying ones that are lean and have a lower fat content is a healthier protein option. Processed meats loaded with preservatives, such as hot dogs, bacon, sausages, spam, and deli meats, are very unhealthy choices. Turkey and other white meats that are not well processed are better meat alternatives.

Fish is a great option; however, some fish contains more toxins than others, so researching where the fish came from, and how many toxins it's likely to contain will help you decide the better option. Normally, a larger fish has more toxins, but it also depends on where the fish lived and the conditions of its habitat.

Wild-caught fish is a healthier option than farm-raised fish. This is because wild-caught fish swim around eating mostly natural things. Farm-raised fish tend to eat what's given to them. Although, some farm-raised fish tend to have more omega-3 fatty acids due to being fed fortified foods—they can also be a more sustainable option as the world's resources continue to diminish.

Many people don't like the taste of fish at all, but it can be prepared in many ways to taste great, so you don't need to let a fishy taste discourage you. A good recipe can make all the difference.

Nuts are also a great option; they have an extensive nutrient profile and are a great source of good fats and protein. Some nuts are better than others though, peanuts (not actually nuts) have higher saturated fat and phosphorus while walnuts and pecans are mostly unsaturated fats.

Unsalted and organic nuts makes for an even healthier option.

Fats

Fats are also very important to your health, yet many people associate them with weight gain and therefore may not be consuming healthy amounts. Fat is another building block for tissues as it makes up your cell walls, which is called a cell membrane in humans and other animals. Fats also help you absorb vitamins, so eating them with vegetables can be helpful. For example, putting olive oil on a salad can help you absorb vitamin A.

Fats also give you energy, as they are a significant source of fuel. Fats also come in healthy and unhealthy versions which are readily available to you. The unhealthiest types of fatty foods contain trans fats, commonly found in fried foods, some processed snacks such as cookies and cakes, and some margarines.

Saturated fats also carry health risks and are found in red meat and dairy products.

Replacing as many of these unhealthy fats with healthy unsaturated fats is a great way to get this very important macronutrient. You can find them in foods such as flaxseeds, nuts, and fatty fish. Extra-virgin olive oil is a great substitute for other oils and butter. The extra-virgin version is also high in polyphenols, the antioxidant discussed in the first chapter.

Avocados are also a great source of healthy fat—they have an extensive nutrient profile and can be eaten as part of any meal at any time of day.

Micronutrients

The macronutrients mentioned so far contain some of the micronutrients you need such as vitamin B and iron, but to get a proper nutritional diet that supports your health, you need to consume multiple servings of fruits and vegetables daily. These foods have lots of vitamins and minerals, and great amounts of fiber and water.

Vegetables are low in calories, so they can also benefit weight loss if they replace other high calorie foods. They can also be more filling, so choosing to eat them primarily, or before high calorie foods, can result in you consuming less calories in total.

Some excellent vegetables to consider are green leafy vegetables such as lettuce and spinach. These are great options for salads and smoothies. Sweet potatoes were already mentioned, but other root vegetables such as garlic, ginger, and onions have many health benefits and their flavors make meals taste amazing.

Cruciferous vegetables are among the healthiest for most people in moderation, this includes broccoli, cabbage, and brussels sprouts. They contain many vitamins and nutrients, and some possibly also have antiaging effects due to their antioxidants, which have the ability to repair DNA. There is a lot of research being done on these vegetables for their antiaging potential, so it's good to look out for new research on them.

As with anything in life, you need things in moderation—it's the same with vegetables. Too much of one vegetable may be harmful for you. You might not be able to eat certain vegetables at all, or only in low amounts. Some vegetables can inhibit the absorption of other nutrients, so pairing them correctly with other vegetables and foods is essential—especially for vegans and vegetarians who rely on a mostly plant diet.

Understanding Nutrition

Additionally, if you have a disorder or are on certain medication, such blood thinners, you should work with your doctors to determine which vegetables are best for you.

Vegetables are disliked by many, but it's often because they haven't yet had the right type, mixture, or cooked them in a way they enjoy. There are also a vast variety of spices that both promote health and make vegetables taste amazing. Many people that were not previously vegetable eaters start after they've had that perfect recipe, and they go on to enjoy many health benefits because of it.

It's healthier to eat a variety of vegetables versus eating the same ones every day, which is another reason why having lists is helpful: They are adaptable and keep you organized with your food choices.

Mushrooms

Mushrooms are in the vegetable category, but these are fungi and not actually plants. Many are edible and very healthy for you. Mushrooms are low in calories and contain antioxidants, vitamins, and fiber. They also contain ergothioneine, an antioxidant that is able to slow cell damage and decrease cancer risks, and selenium, an antioxidant that can decrease inflammation and enhance your immune system.

Additionally, mushrooms are a great food source for the good gut bacteria that are essential to your health and wellbeing. Mushrooms are also commonly disliked, particularly for the texture, so you may be missing these potential benefits. If the texture is an issue, cut them down and add them to a mixture of other foods to make them easier to eat.

Some mushrooms are poisonous and have other effects, so you should be aware of which ones are safe. If you're trying to maximize the health benefits of mushrooms, learning which are higher in antioxidants will help you chose which have the most potential.

However, most edible mushrooms have great health benefits regardless.

Fruits

Fruits have amazing nutritional value and they taste great. They are an excellent alternative to other desserts such as ice cream and cakes.

Fruits are mainly water and contain fiber, so their sugar content is not as harmful as those foods with added sugars. They also have many vitamins, minerals, and polyphenols. Fruits can be a very healthy option to achieve proper nutrition and replace high calorie desserts.

Berries are low in carbohydrates and are packed with nutrients and antioxidants. Strawberries, blueberries, blackberries, and raspberries have extensive nutritional value and are all low in calories.

A great way to get both fruits and vegetables into your day is to make a smoothie. Smoothies are convenient, taste great, and you can choose the exact ingredients you wish to consume. They are also easy to switch up—you could have kale one day and spinach the next. You can also add in important omega foods such as flaxseeds.

Researching smoothie recipes or making your own can be a fun and easy way to meet your nutritional needs. You could even add protein powder to make them a post-workout drink.

It can be difficult to achieve the right consistency in smoothies; it can take time to get right. There's no need to feel discouraged if the first couple don't come out great. As always, moderation is important, and fruits may not be for everyone. Many conditions and diseases require you to be very strategic about your food choices. It's important to your health to be conscientious and educated about what's right for you.

Snacks

It's very common to consume snacks each day. Unfortunately, most snacks are highly processed and contain large amounts of sodium, simple sugars, and other additives. They can also cause you to eat less during your complete meals or you might even skip a meal.

Extensive marketing pushes snacks as great, and even healthy, foods for you for in between meals, but they are often unnecessary. Your body may desire snacks if your meals lack proper nutrition. If you eat more whole foods, you may find it easier to get to your next meal without needing to snack.

For some people, however, snacks help them feel energized between meals, and this makes sense for them. Some diseases, for example, require you to eat smaller meals spread throughout the day, as well as snacks, to avoid health problems. It's important to *listen* to your body to determine whether you need more energy or if you may be lacking certain vitamins and minerals.

If snacking is necessary, the produce section is a much healthier place to look for them versus the grocery isle. Fruits, vegetables, and nuts make for very healthy and delicious snacks.

Drinks

What you drink can be a major cause of low energy and health problems. Certain drinks are marketed as natural and healthy options because of a few trivial ingredients; looking at a food label will quickly reveal that they have extensive sugar and sodium as well as artificial colors and flavors.

Even natural flavors can contain chemicals.

Artificial sweeteners are also not great alternatives to sugar as they can signal to the brain that food is coming, which can increase appetite and prompt you to eat, getting the calories regardless. These food additives are permissible by the FDA in certain amounts, but since they have the potential to contribute to weight gain and ongoing studies are working to determine whether these chemicals are safe, it's better to avoid them altogether.

As previously mentioned, water is amazing for hydration—replace your sugary drinks with water and after a while, you will likely find you don't want to drink them anymore. Interestingly, people who try sugary drinks after consuming only water for a while find it difficult to tolerate them and wonder how they ever did in the first place.

Water is the healthiest option, but even this must be properly prepared.

Filtering water is important to remove dangerous contaminants. Additionally, some plastics can leach harmful chemicals into your water. This can also increase when given time and certain temperatures. Glass containers are therefore the safest option available and also maintain the original taste better.

Tea can be a healthy substitute and has long been thought to have many health benefits—at least in moderation. Tea is a low-calorie option with very low caffeine levels. It also comes in extensive varieties, and it's fun to try new ones. Some contain natural and artificial flavors, and many have sugars and sweeteners that you can determine from reading their ingredient and nutrition labels.

If you're not too sensitive to caffeine, coffee can be a low-calorie drink. There is a lot of back and forth research discussing how healthy it can be for you, but coffee, like tea, also contains antioxidants which decrease the damaging effects of free radicals. These drinks become a problem when you add sweeteners and milk—they then instantly

Understanding Nutrition

become unhealthy. Look for tea and coffee that is organic for the ultimate health benefits.

Good Bacteria

Bacteria often get a bad reputation because of the small percentage that cause disease and illness. However, you cannot survive without them. You have a unique microbiome in your skin, digestive tract, and lungs, as well as other areas of your body that is symbiotic with you.

You provide your bacteria with nutrients and a home to survive, and they provide you benefits such as improved digestion, better immunity, and they also produce vitamins and protect against harmful bacteria. They have also been linked to your mood.

If you treat your bacteria well, they treat you well.

To encourage their survival and the important benefits they provide you, a good diet is crucial. Conveniently, the foods that are good for your health such as fruits, vegetables, and mushrooms are good for your microbiome as well. The fiber in these foods is a prebiotic, which are plant fibers gut bacteria can use for nutrition. Just the same, the harmful foods that are bad for you can be harmful to your bacteria, too.

Eating fried foods, for example, feed the bad bacteria and allow them to increase their numbers and fight for more control in your gut; this can counterbalance and poorly distribute your good bacteria. This is called dysbiosis and can result in symptoms such as fatigue, digestive issues, and poor mood as well as lead to health problems.

Sometimes, you can wipe out your good bacteria during antibiotic treatments. They can be added back by consuming certain foods with live cultures and properly manufactured probiotics. Keeping your gut bacteria happy and healthy will allow them to do their part for your health.

Food Preparation

Some foods are inherently unhealthy, but it can also be the way they are prepared. Many illnesses and diseases are a result of this. Most people know to wash their hands and rinse foods very well.

Washing cutting boards and tools very well to remove all microorganisms is also important.

Checking foods for decay and spoilage is necessary because if they sit for great lengths of time, they can become less nutritional and cause illness.

Foods that require cooking are most nutritional within a few hours after cooking them. Foods should also be cooked to their proper temperatures to kill harmful microorganisms and should not be overcooked. Using a thermometer is a better choice than trusting your gut.

Using high heat during cooking, such as when frying or barbecuing, can reduce nutrients and convert some organic compounds into chemical ones. For example, creatine can be converted to a group of chemical compounds called heterocyclic amines (HCAs) during high heat cooking. HCAs can be cancerous to you in high amounts. Ensuring you uphold safe and comprehensive food preparation will reduce your chances of getting sick.

Fasting

Fasting is not something new, but it has been getting more and more attention recently. Many studies show support for this type of eating. Fasting claims to lead to weight loss, decreased inflammation, and even the possibility of slowing down aging. There are also some health benefits for longer-term fasting that state you can recycle dead cells and other things that accumulate in your body.

It can reduce your eating window, so it has the potential to reduce the number of calories you consume. The basic idea is to skip a meal and eat only in a six-to-eight-hour window. More advanced versions have people eating one meal a day, or going multiple days without eating, only consuming water, coffee, and tea. This reduction in meals can certainly lower calorie counts if you stick to it, but it runs the risk of leading you to consume large meals at once or to give up on the diet and return to bad eating habits, or possibly eating worse than before.

If you choose to fast, first speak to your doctor about it and be careful to watch for signs of dizziness, poor concentration, weakness, or anything else new and report it to your primary physician.

You have always been told to eat three meals a day and snacks, but as you develop further understanding, things can change, and there may be ways that you can achieve substantially better health and fitness than ever before from doing so.

Reducing Food Costs

Food costs are a big factor for many people, especially in times of inflation, shortages, and economic recession. Buying food in bulk decreases costs significantly. Your lists can also include which stores have the best prices for individual or bulk items in order to keep you organized. Buying as many things as possible at once will also reduce the number of trips you have to make to the store.

Vegetables last longer when refrigerated, so taking them out a couple at a time will reduce their chance of spoiling before use. Frozen vegetables are generally priced much lower than fresh ones, and they're still a healthy choice as they're typically frozen quickly so that they retain their nutrients.

However, some frozen vegetables have sugar added to them while being processed. You can determine this from looking at the food label. Organic frozen vegetables can be difficult to find, so you may want to consider this, too. Frozen fruits are also typically a great cost-to-quantity ratio, and last much longer when frozen.

Organization

As mentioned at the start of this chapter, it's very helpful to be organized. This will increase the likelihood you make healthy meals and decrease the chances you'll snack on unhealthy foods. Food, meals, shopping, and recipe lists can really help.

Foods you research can be added or removed from these lists; this allows the lists to adapt over time, making decisions so much easier. You can also find ways to make meals much quicker, so it isn't as much work to make them after a long day. Fast and premade meals are heavily processed, so learning to make meals quickly at home can help you to avoid these.

A restaurant list is also important so you know the best local options available to you. Eventually, all the foods you have in your home will be well-vetted, easy to make, and delicious. Any time you wander from your lists, they will be there when you come back and you can pick up from where you left off. A well-designed nutrition strategy will save money and make healthier eating so much easier.

Understanding What's "Healthy"

Making your food lists and knowing what's healthy for you can be very challenging when one source says it's good for you and another says that it's not.

Understanding Nutrition

If you can see a registered dietician, they can provide you some lists to help you get started. If you have health problems and are on certain medications, you may need to follow certain diet guidelines from your doctor and stick to them the best you can. But if you're doing your own research, there are some important things to consider that will make determining healthy food choices much easier.

It's always good to learn to read food labels as best as possible. Learning what ingredients are in foods and how many calories they contain can help you to be more aware of what and how much you consume. You may also want to be at least somewhat skeptical about any foods that people claim are "healthy for you."

For example, you can type "are tomatoes good for you?" into Google, and it may result in information such as they are "very healthy" and packed full of "nutrients, fiber, and antioxidants." But then, if you type in, "are tomatoes bad for you?" you may get information stating that they are "nightshades, inflammatory, the skin and seeds are harmful, and they can cause allergies in certain people."

Unfortunately, there is an overwhelming amount of conflicting information available, which is what makes things so difficult. To add to that, some sources that have stated before that something is healthy may state later that it isn't. This can make it difficult to know what to choose for your health.

There are some things you can do to improve your research if you're trying to determine what's healthy for you.

When researching about a food, you may want to do so with an open mind and look at information that both supports and combats it before comparing both. Individual studies on foods and food additives are sometimes unreliable and steer you in the wrong direction.

However, a meta-analysis compares multiple studies, and data that stacks up is more reliable than just one study. It's also important to make sure your research comes from a credible expert in the field.

When determining healthy options, update your food lists and make new recipes often. These lists can build over a lifetime, so you don't need to pressure yourself to make too many changes at once—this can do more harm than good.

Making Changes Conscientiously

It's important to implement changes slowly so your body can adapt. Changing your diet too quickly can cause unwanted side effects. It's also important to check with your doctor before starting a new diet to determine whether it complements your health. Nutrition needs are different for everyone and increasing your individual activity level can mean you have different caloric and hydration needs as well.

Setting goals and making changes to meet them will improve your health and fitness. Monitoring how you feel along the way is important to be sure you are doing it well. It's very important to understand that just because some foods are unhealthy for you, they may be all that you currently have access to.

Eliminating foods entirely is never the solution to better health, it's better to replace them with healthier foods.

You may not be able to afford healthy foods for weeks, months, or even years. You should transition when it becomes an option for you. You, and the people you are responsible for, still need calories to get through your day. Making health changes necessitates doing so conscientiously.

Conclusion

Eating well may require removing things that you really like from your diet, but having more energy, better moods, and avoiding expensive and unpleasant health problems will allow you to really enjoy life.

It may take some time to see results, but they will come with the right amount of effort.

You may drift away from your health goals during busy projects or while traveling but getting back to them quickly is much easier when you are organized and know what you want. Having better health and fitness can make an amazing difference in your life, and you can certainly make progress soon after you begin.

PART III

Fitness

To achieve great fitness levels, you need to dedicate more time and effort to exercise than you typically would for just your health. You also need to be even more concerned about your diet and hydration as these affect your health and ability to achieve fitness goals.

It also requires exercising often and changing workouts periodically to maintain and improve performance. You may also need motivation or determination to keep you consistent.

Major muscle groups need dedicated workout time to develop, or they reduce. Different types of workouts will have different results depending on what you wish to pursue. You may want to focus on endurance and power, others may want to increase strength and muscle size.

You may want something in between, or both.

Warmups and stretches will help improve your mobility, flexibility, and workout results. They also help you to avoid injury, setbacks, and discouragement. Any strain or pain is a sign your stretches, or exercises, are not being performed properly. It's also important to understand

WELL-ROUNDED

your limits, health conditions, disabilities, and injuries so you know which exercises are safe for you to perform.

There are many precautions you can take to help you avoid problems; exercises come with varying levels of risk. You will need to monitor your health and watch for the development of symptoms.

Your workout area should be clean and organized to avoid injury. If you address your safety and stay dedicated to fitness, you will look and feel amazing, perform at greater ability, and have better focus, energy, and strength. The time you put into your fitness yields results and increases motivation and dedication.

You will be more confident, feel great, and become your best self.

CHAPTER 8

Motivation & Obstacles

Achieving a good level of fitness requires consistency, so you may need to find ways to retain motivation and remove obstacles. Motivation can be understood in a few ways: As external influence, self-motivation, or determination.

External influence includes things such as a deadline at work or wanting to look good for summer—this often enhances dedication, too.

Self-motivation can simply be bringing music to the gym. You basically persuade yourself to be more motivated to exercise for a certain length of time, and you do so by using something you think will help.

Determination can also motivate you, but this is more like a drive: You are compelled to accomplish something without ever giving up unless one day you change your mind.

Other sources may explain this differently, but this explanation may help you identify opportunities to find and make use of motivation. Lack of motivation can be an obstacle to getting fit, but there are many others, too.

WELL-ROUNDED

Obstacles make it difficult to achieve your goals or even to get them started.

Others include: Time, money, equipment, knowledge, location, and disabilities among others. There are many things you can do to confront these challenges and overcome them to accomplish your goals.

Organization, as mentioned, is a great way to free up more time. Working to improve your finances can allow you access to a gym or to increase your home equipment. Learning to work around disabilities and improving your knowledge about exercise can also help. There are many ways that you can overcome your obstacles and find a place for fitness training in your life.

Determination

Determination is not triggered easily, or even intentionally, for the most part. If it was, everyone would be successful. Determination provides you with relentless energy and focus to accomplish a goal. Although it improves your life by pushing you in a good direction, it can lead to obsessiveness and harm, too.

Regarding fitness, determination can push you to exercise every day, and for great lengths of time. This means you'll see results quickly and will feel great, healthy, and highly capable. Conversely, it can drive you too hard and you may sacrifice areas of your health because of it. Outside of fitness, it can drive you in your career and in life to be very successful.

In contrast, it can drive you to make poor decisions that hurt you financially.

Determination is not always controllable, but if you can, use it to motivate you towards healthy goals. Determination often comes out of nowhere, so it's important to take advantage of it as soon as it presents itself. If it's harming you, or others are finding your actions concerning,

Motivation & Obstacles

see your primary physician to determine where you can get the right guidance and support.

When people are determined to do something, there's very little that can stop them. But if your goals are something harmful to you, you may see only hardship.

Motivation From an External Influence

Sometimes you get motivated due to a deadline at work, or because you want to get into better shape before a wedding. These things can influence you to be motivated and set goals that you wouldn't normally. These sources of motivation can also be good or bad depending on the circumstances.

Motivation can help you get started right away, which is healthy because it means you're becoming engaged with your goal, or it can be unhealthy and cause stress and panic. If you put too much pressure on yourself and don't take proper care, it will also impede your thinking and planning.

Some stress is very good as it will help you focus, but you should manage it carefully. Plan your steps beforehand so when you're motivated to start working toward your goals, you can spread the work evenly with specific objectives. This will reduce your stress and likely let you achieve a better outcome.

Furthermore, if you do achieve something fantastic such as weight loss or getting into better shape, you are then in a great position to maintain it. Getting started is often the hardest part, but maintenance is generally much easier once you know what works. When you feel motivated, you can use it to improve yourself and sustain your results.

Self-Motivation

If you want to accomplish something new, you typically need to motivate yourself.

You may be prompted by outside factors, or you may just want to accomplish something you want personally. These factors can sometimes get you started to establish an actual goal to work towards. You can use the goal itself to motivate you because each time you think about it, you may develop the desire to pursue it—it's the reason you're putting in the work in the first place.

Pertaining to fitness, there's no shortage of amazing benefits you can use as your goal. You can do it for your health, weight loss, or to tone up and look great. You may also want better performance or to get better at a specific sport, which you can achieve by increasing your strength, power, or endurance.

These goals can motivate you to get started and continue working towards them. You can then develop habits that take over. Alternatively, you may need to keep thinking about your goal to motivate you further. If your goal no longer motivates you entirely, there are many other things you can use for self-motivation.

Warmups and Music

You need to find things that motivate you to keep you interested in your pursuits. There are many things you can use; it's helpful to have multiple different options. Mentioned in a previous chapter, just getting started may be all it takes.

In terms of exercise, doing your warmups and getting your blood pumping will give you an energy boost that helps give you momentum and get yourself into a good mindset for the main workout phase.

Motivation & Obstacles

As mentioned before, you can also use music to stay motivated. Try using different types of music depending on the type of exercise you're doing: You could play relaxing music before a yoga workout, or uplifting and inspirational music to energize and get you into a good mindset for running and weightlifting. Music can increase your focus, energy, and mood, and has extensive variety, so there will never be a shortage of songs you can choose from.

Distractions Keep You Going

Television can also work very well. That is why you often see television sets hanging on the wall at your gym. They don't typically work to motivate you, but rather to distract you so you can continue working out without thinking about the challenge of exercise.

Time will pass quicker and you will be able to exercise for longer because of this distraction.

You could always watch a TV show or the news while you work out and accomplish two things at once. This may also keep you off the couch later when you would normally catch up on these shows. The downside of television during a workout is that it can lead to injury if you're not concentrating—it's best to pair it with muscle memory exercises such as running on a treadmill or exercise bikes.

Therefore, this is useful when you're trying to increase your endurance or lose weight, which both require long durations of exercise.

Following Your Progress

Another great method is to take before and after pictures so you can track your progress. If you're committed to exercise and stick to a good diet, you're going to see results.

It's like cleaning the garage.

If you go in there and work on it every day, it's going to look better each time. This is the same with diet and exercise: It delivers results. If you take a few pictures of yourself before you get started and then each subsequent month that you're sticking to your plan, you're likely to see dramatic changes.

Not only can you can be proud of this, but it will help you stay engaged with your workout plan and inspire you to try even harder. You may notice weight loss, more muscle, or a toned physique.

This is a form of positive reinforcement; seeing results from your hard work is very rewarding.

You may also get compliments from others who notice your changes and congratulate you on your progress. Likewise, when you have your annual physical and your physician finds improvement in your health, they may also show you further encouragement. Diet and exercise are hard work, so seeing results is a great reward for your efforts.

Finding Inspiration

Getting inspired by others is a great way to find motivation. Just as you can motivate others, they too can motivate you. There are many people that you can follow online to inspire you to keep exercising and working hard to achieve your fitness goals.

There are people such as exercise enthusiasts, actors, friends, fitness professionals, and many others who are very passionate about exercise. Many of these people have achieved incredible accomplishments and advocate for others to achieve their ambitions, too.

Finding someone with similar goals to you and learning what you can from them may both motivate you and give you new techniques to achieve even greater results. You can also do this by finding a workout

Motivation & Obstacles

buddy, someone who you can exercise with. You can also support each other's goals.

Everyone else needs exercise, too. You may have friends or family members that would benefit from exercising more. You can team up with them so that you can motivate each other to meet your goals. You may even be able to combine workout equipment or play sports with them, as we tend to push ourselves harder when competing with someone.

Likewise, you could join a sports team, which may really increase your performance so you can play at greater ability. Sports are great ways to meet people, get ideas to further improve, and are another source of motivation.

Changing up Your Workout

You can stay engaged with your workouts and keep them fun by regularly changing them up so that you don't lose interest in your routine. This is important when you hit a plateau and become unable to advance to a greater performance.

The only way to move past a plateau is to make a particular exercise more difficult. This will be discussed further in later chapters, but it works well to change your workouts periodically so that they are not boring or repetitive. It's important to find something at your current level instead of something too difficult or too easy. Working your way up to more challenging workouts will help you avoid injury and discouragement.

Looking for something that you find fun and enjoyable is also important. If you are performing a workout plan that you just don't like, there are many others you may find more interesting. For example, you could try running outside instead of on a treadmill to change things up.

The great part about exercise is that it can be changed anytime you find new ideas, and there is no shortage of possibilities. If you have limitations or health conditions, you can ask your doctor or personal trainer for a new workout plan if you lose interest in one. The people that happen to be the most committed to exercise and fitness are either determined, or they just love doing it. So, find ways to enjoy exercise to make it a regular part of your life for time to come.

Obstacles

Following the same exercise routine can make it difficult to stay motivated for sure. This is also an obstacle, and one that you can adapt to by changing your workout plan.

There are many other obstacles that will either impede your ability to improve or discourage you. One such thing is time; you only have so much time in a day to address your responsibilities.

Fitness training requires a lot more strategizing because you need to stay consistent and dedicate a good amount of time each day to progress. This is another reason why motivation to exercise is important: When you're motivated to do something, you will find the time for it. As mentioned, organization and creating a good schedule will really help you free up more time in your day.

You really need a good plan to make fitness possible.

Working out in the morning has many advantages and is generally more realistic as you can exercise before anyone else is awake, so you have less distractions. Working out in the morning also energizes you for your day and may make it seem like you have more time. You also may have less aches and pains from work because your muscles were warmed up and you increased the functioning and mobility of your joints.

Motivation & Obstacles

It also benefits you to at least warm up and stretch before work anyways because of benefits that will be discussed in the next chapter. Additionally, working out at home can overcome a lot of obstacles that might be in your way of going to a gym, so investing in workout equipment might be what you need to stay consistent.

Fitness Costs

For some, money is an issue. There are costs for gym memberships, workout equipment, increased food costs, and many other new expenses depending on what you want. But it doesn't have to be an obstacle to achieving great fitness. Having good money management skills and planning for these expenses will stop them from being hindrances.

If you need to, start small and work your way up when your finances improve.

You could start working out at home or at the park. Many people begin by using furniture around their house as workout equipment. You can use a good sturdy chair for dips to improve your triceps. You can perform pushups and sit-ups without any equipment. Carpet can work well as an alternative to an exercise mat.

Cost is more of a discouragement than a complete obstacle. Many people achieve incredible fitness levels without spending any money on workout equipment, gym memberships, or workout clothes. The only essential cost would be if you required more water and calories to meet your fitness needs.

Eventually you may want some of these other things, such as new equipment or getting access to a gym, to advance your fitness and to keep you interested and engaged in your workouts.

As long as you have the money to address your calorie needs, cost doesn't have to hold you back from getting started and well on your way to amazing fitness.

WELL-ROUNDED

Fitness Knowledge

Your existing fitness knowledge or disability can certainly be obstacles to achieving fitness. However, they too can be overcome by improving your understanding and changing your mindset to develop yourself.

There are extensive fitness workouts and training regimens online and in books. Online, you can find a range of videos by professionals on everything from guided meditation and yoga to instructions on strength and power training. These guides explain how to properly perform exercises and will help you work toward more advanced levels.

You could also find personal trainers at your local gym to teach you basic and advanced workout plans. There is no shortage of resources for learning to improve your fitness.

Finding time in your day and throughout your week and implementing a workout plan will help you increase your fitness levels further and further. If you don't like a certain exercise, there are many others that you can try.

Another challenge is working around injuries, health conditions, and disabilities. You can be born with limitations, or develop them during your life. This can severely restrict your ability to exercise and improve. However, there are incredible stories of people working around these obstacles and achieving remarkable fitness.

Some get their exercise from swimming, bed and chair exercises, or specially-designed workout equipment. People with disabilities compete in sports such as wheelchair basketball, fencing, and more.

People with certain limits can still achieve great fitness when they find something that interests them and which they can become passionate about. There are also many professionals that specialize in creating workouts for people with health problems, injuries, or disabilities to achieve great fitness and improve their health.

Getting information about exercise programs and activities and looking for something that's interesting to you can help you find something you might really enjoy and want to pursue.

Getting Started with Activity and Staying Engaged

There are many things that stand in your way of improving your fitness and enjoying the many benefits that result from it. This can include yourself and your desire to exercise and bring fitness into your life. However, the world of exercise and fitness is extensive, so learning about different workout routines and activities will help you eventually come across something that piques your interest.

There are different workouts such as martial arts, yoga, and Pilates, and even fun sports such as kayaking, archery, and bowling that can get you to be more active. This will help you to increase your energy and interest levels to begin full body workouts that target your muscles, cardiovascular system, joints, and bones.

You can then set goals and use motivational techniques to stay consistent.

Even with great dedication, you can still fall off your routine and find it difficult to get back to it. As a result, you may lose some of the improvements you previously achieved. Your endurance may decrease, and your weight begin to rise. Yet, your body will be ready to get back to it when you are.

Sometimes, unavoidable changes in your schedule, traveling to other places, getting injured, or having less time will mean you fall off your workout routine.

However, you can adapt to changes in your life to stay connected to your fitness and get back to your workouts as soon as possible.

If it's lack of desire, setting new goals and changing up the workout are great ways to stay engaged. If there are changes to your schedule, you may want to strategize your week to find gaps that you can use for exercise or have a plan in mind for when you can get back to it again.

It's important that when returning to exercise you reduce the duration and intensity. You can get back to where you were before relatively quickly, but the first week or two should be taken slowly. It only takes a couple weeks to lose some ability and put yourself at risk for injury.

If you go months or years without exercise, you need to take it much slower and build back up.

Many people return to their workout at their normal intensity and injure themselves, creating further setbacks and discouragement. It's certainly fine to halve your intensity and duration until you get back to your usual ability, and any plans you had to keep advancing.

Your body will remember, but it needs time to regain its abilities.

Conclusion

Good fitness will come with time and dedication. Determining your interests is all you need to get started to pursue your goals. The most consistent people are those that just love what they do. They don't really see it as a chore—it's their passion, and they look forward to doing it. The results are just a bonus.

There will be many obstacles, but you can overcome them. You are a creative and capable problem solver. You can accomplish so many things you wouldn't initially believe possible.

You do this best when you build your ability over time and stay consistent.

Motivation & Obstacles

Fitness is worth taking on this challenge for as it does so many great things for your body and mind. You become healthier, feel better, and have greater physical ability. Knowing that there will be difficulties and learning to overcome them will allow you to stay connected to your fitness and achieve great things.

CHAPTER 9

Warmups & Stretching

Preparing for the main workout phase primes your muscles and joints for the work you expect them to do. It's also important to avoid injury and limit soreness as these things can deter you from future workouts.

A warmup will reduce stiffness in the body and bring nutrients and oxygen to the muscles for energy and stretching will increase your range of motion and flexibility, which will allow you to target a greater range of the muscles you're working on.

Post-workout benefits of these include faster recovery and reduced soreness, so you're ready for your next workout. A proper warmup and cool down are also important to safely raise and lower your heart rate and to reduce any possible side effects.

Additionally, warmups and stretching are great ways to prepare you for your job among other activities. If you feel achy or have lower back or neck pain after working, you may be able to eliminate or reduce these problems with warmups and stretching before work. You can also benefit from warmups and stretching on non-workout days for improved flexibility, to reduce soreness, and speed up recovery.

These preparations will provide extensive benefits that will allow you to achieve better fitness from exercise and increase your ability. Unfortunately, many people stop prioritizing warmups over time—this is understandable, as you only have so much time and want to get to the exercises you feel will provide the best results. However, warmups are very beneficial, and there are ways to keep them interesting.

Spice Up Your Warmups

As mentioned, your warmup is crucial to getting your body and brain ready to exercise, which will mean you're more focused and feel more committed to seeing your workout through. The warmup should especially target the muscles you plan to use during your exercise and should take around ten minutes.

For cardio, try running in place or jogging slowly until your body warms up. Each type of exercise has different complimentary warmups that will help you achieve results. Whenever you begin a new workout, it's important to know which warmups compliment them.

It's common to perform typical warmups such as jumping jacks, jump rope, or just running in place. Yet, there are many ways that you can spice up your warmups to make them more interesting. One way to do this is to practice martial arts—this way, you can learn to better defend yourself and warm up at the same time.

It's important to keep in mind that these moves also need a warmup and stretching beforehand too, but if you start light and fluid, and increase from there, it works fantastically. Use slow, flowing movements until you're warmed up, then stretch to help transition to the main workout phase.

Warmups & Stretching

Performing about ten minutes or so of martial arts (involving punches and blocks) on upper body workout days is a warmup for the torso, back, and upper extremities. Similarly, if it's a lower body workout day, try kicks.

Running in place for a couple minutes and trying out these martial arts moves can help you to build skill and accuracy.

Another fun warmup is dancing, whether you're practicing existing moves or learning for the first time. You can even extend your warmup for more time to learn moves. If you already know how to dance, you can just get started. Otherwise, watching a few videos beforehand will allow you to find some moves to practice and improve over time.

Once you have mastered certain movements, try adding new ones. You can also compare yourself with professionals to be sure you perform them correctly.

Dancing and martial arts are fun and fantastic ways to warm up your body for your main workout. As with any form of exercise, it's important to create plenty of space so as not to cause injury or break anything. These are great ways to keep your warmups interesting and to build new skills at the same time.

Light Activity as a Warmup

Going for a light run is a great way to warm up and improve circulation before you stretch and begin your main workout—it's all you really need to get warmed up. While jogging, you can strategize about the workout you plan to do to improve efficiency.

Even just playing with a ball around the yard works, such as kicking a soccer ball, or some light basketball. This offers enjoyment and can help keep you interested and more consistent with your warmups. It's better to avoid getting into an aggressive game before you've had a chance to really warm up though—any injury, however minimal, can really be a setback.

Additionally, too long of a warmup can cause you to fatigue and may compromise your ability and desire for the entire main workout phase. Aiming for about ten minutes or so is generally enough to get you ready to work out. People tend to reduce or skip their warmups when they're too routine, so make it fun and interesting and switch it up when needed.

There are plenty of warmup exercises to choose from, but you will need to figure out which ones pair well with your specific workout.

Stretching

Stretching can also become very routine and cause you to become indifferent and put in less effort or skip it entirely. In addition to avoiding injury and setback, stretching has amazing advantages.

Stretching will help you get more oxygen and nutrients to tissues that really benefit from it, and your muscles and joints will become more flexible and can increase their range. This also helps you build more muscle strength during your main workout, therefore improving your performance and increasing your fitness level.

Stretching is valuable for mitigating muscle stiffness and reducing post-exercise soreness. Incorporating a warm-up and engaging in full-body stretches or yoga can alleviate tightness and discomfort, which will help you feel and perform better.

Importance of Properly Stretching

It's helpful to have a list of stretches that correlate with the workout you plan to do. Quality workout plans that people purchase or get from their trainers should include which stretches, warmups, and cool downs to do alongside each workout. They should also be explicit about how to perform them properly.

Stretching should target the muscles you plan to work out or include a full body stretch. Neck and core stretches are needed in all workouts—there is typically some straining on the neck and back in every exercise, so they're vulnerable to injury during physical activity.

The body should be completely warmed up before stretching. Don't rush your stretches, and don't stretch until you feel pain—only tightness. Fifteen to thirty seconds per stretch is ideal, however you may need to adjust this time for painful areas.

Breathing is also important to relieve stress and extend further. These are the important parts of stretching that allow you the most benefits and reduce the potential for injury and setbacks. You can also go back and target problematic areas. For example, if you feel shoulder pain when attempting pushups, instead of pushing through the pain, stand up and do some arm circles.

This will get some rotation going in the region, allowing the shoulder to open more and release any tension before going back to the workout.

Pain during exercise, other than soreness from a prior workout, tells you there's a problem or that you're performing the exercise incorrectly. If this happens, stretching or correcting how you exercise can solve the problem.

Types of Stretching

The previous information is meant to increase your understanding of the benefits of stretching that you'll lose should you remove them from your workouts, and the risks you'll increase by doing so. But there are many more advantages to stretching if it is done well. There are different types of stretches; two will be discussed here.

The first is static stretching, which is good for many reasons, such as flexibility. This type of stretching is basic and part of most workouts because of its range of benefits. Static stretches extend the muscles to give you more range. They also stretch and loosen the joints and surrounding tissues, improve your flexibility, and allow more blood circulation to the area, making them great for injury prevention and improving ability.

You can also use static stretches after workouts to relax tight muscles and reduce soreness.

Another type is dynamic stretching, which also has many benefits—primarily, range of motion. Dynamic stretching can increase joint mobility, which decreases possibility of injury and allows you better ability during and after exercise.

Static stretching can improve your performance with flexibility and increased muscle; dynamic stretching can help you move quicker and more freely.

Dynamic stretches, as the name suggests, are continuous movements that allow your joints to go through a full range of motions and are great pre-workout to loosen your muscles and joints. They can also be done during your cool down.

During dynamic stretching, it's better to avoid dramatic and aggressive movements to prevent injury. Warming up and performing static and dynamic stretches on non-workout days can also speed up your recovery and can be very relaxing.

Cooldowns

Exercise raises your heart rate very high, especially during high intensity workouts such as plyometrics and running as they work your largest

Warmups & Stretching

muscle groups: The legs and glutes. Therefore, it's also important to do a proper cool down after any exercise.

If your heart is beating very quickly and you suddenly just stop exercising, it can make you dizzy or faint, which can cause injury. Cooldowns only take a few minutes, so they are not much of a time investment.

They are also important for a few reasons.

In addition to reducing the stress on your heart, a proper cooldown aids in the smoother transition of your muscles and joints, promoting increased flexibility and reducing stiffness and soreness after exercise. Additionally, it may lower the likelihood of experiencing muscle cramps.

Walking, or another low intensity exercise, and dynamic stretching work great to bring your heart rate down slowly. Following this up with some static stretching will then help you complete your workout with the greatest benefits.

Warmups and Stretching Before Work and Activities

Warmups and stretches reduce stress and prepare your body for physical activity.

Additionally, some businesses also ask their employees to perform warmups and stretches before working their shift. This is a great suggestion as you're about to enter a long duration of activity, sitting, or repetitiveness.

Stretches are particularly helpful for construction workers, who perform hard labor, or mechanics who do a lot of twisting, turning, and lifting. It also helps for restaurant workers and those standing for great lengths of time. Everyone can really find some benefit from this strategy, such as reduced aches and pains.

It can also help after work, especially if any area of your body is nagging you.

Injuries can also improve much faster using warmups and stretches as well as physical therapy exercises, so it's beneficial to determine which are right for you and to be consistent with them.

Furthermore, warmups and stretching, or performing meditation and yoga on your non-workout days, will build strength, improve circulation, and remove waste from all parts of the body so that you heal and feel much better.

Conclusion

There are many ways to keep warmups and stretches interesting. Benefits such as greater performance are likely why you're improving your fitness in the first place.

Finding ways to enjoy these will help you remain consistent and thorough. If you find that they're getting too routine, there are many suitable alternatives.

Warming up and cooling down are crucial to ensuring you transition safely into and out of exercise, improve your mindset, and give your body the boost of energy it needs.

Stretches will also improve your flexibility and performance. These are essential to improving your fitness levels. You can neglect them over time, but if you remind yourself of their importance and value, you can stay consistent.

CHAPTER 10

Balance & Core

Good balance is important for everyday activities and to avoid injury. Having great balance will improve your fitness and support you in sports and other interests to perform better. Whether you're hiking on the trails, playing sports, climbing a ladder, or just walking around, it's important to have the proper balance for it.

You can incorporate exercises into your workout that maintain and improve your balance. Coordination is an important part of balance, and this, too, can be improved with certain exercises and workouts. Improved balance can help you perform better and avoid injury.

Unfortunately, your ability to balance well can reduce with age, so it's important to maintain it. Balance issues are not always related to strength and coordination, as there are many short- and long-term health conditions that may be the cause of these.

Address any health concerns with your doctor, as they are qualified to help with this. When these conditions are stabilized, you will be better able to maintain and improve your balance using certain exercises.

Building muscles throughout your body can help, but there are some key areas that target balance better.

Strength training in muscle areas such as the legs and core will improve your balance the most.

Poor Balance Due to Health Conditions

You may not be able to address some health conditions that cause poor balance with strength training. These conditions should be followed up by a physician who can address the root problem to let you work to improve your balance with specific strength and coordination exercises.

There are many things that can cause balance issues, such as:

- Infections or inflammation in the inner ear
- Parkinson's disease
- Multiple sclerosis
- Heart problems
- Joint problems
- Drugs and medication

If you experience any of these things, make sure you see a physician to address the cause of your balance problems. They can be very serious in some cases, but there are often treatments available that will reduce your risk of injury and increase your daily performance. That way, you can work on improving yourself when you're at your best.

Maintaining Balance

Balance issues often progress as you age, so it's to your advantage to maintain your balance throughout your life. Maintaining good balance

Balance & Core

can be accomplished by living an active lifestyle. If you're very sedentary and not very active, your balance may decline faster than someone else's.

You can also maintain better balance through routine exercise and building muscle. If you exercise your core and legs each week, this is already helping you improve your balance if you're consistent.

Workouts can be split up and done efficiently to fit into your week better. You can do this by focusing on two areas of the body each day, which will also help to avoid fatigue in one area of the body too quickly. For example, try exercising your legs and shoulders one day and your chest and back another.

You can then choose a separate day for a cardiovascular workout, such as running, which will strengthen many areas in your body as well as improve your heart and lung health. You can also do a day or two dedicated to core training and stretches.

This is an example of efficiently fitting a full body workout into your week to effectively build muscle in the major areas of your body and maintain good balance.

Improving Balance

If you have certain restrictions, speak to your personal trainer and doctor to see if the following balance exercises and workouts can be added. If you have no restrictions, some great exercises and workouts will be discussed in this chapter that you can use to improve your balance to a greater extent.

Some will be exercises that can be added to your routine workout, others are entire workouts in themselves. However, they are all fun and challenging ways to help you improve your balance and performance.

In the health chapter, it was mentioned that there are many health benefits of having good posture. Improving your posture will also help your balance.

Many people who try to improve their balance directly often do so by just using balancing bars to practice. Although this will deliver great results over time, there are exercises that can be added to your workouts that will significantly assist this practice, the results of which will be immediately notable when you go back to the balance bars.

Working to improve your legs and core will help you achieve great balance much faster than just practicing balancing specifically and working on posture. Building muscle in the legs will make you more stable and allow you to control your movement better.

Incorporating at least one lower body workout each week will improve your balance as your legs will get stronger. The main muscle groups to target with your workouts are the quadriceps (front thigh area), hamstrings (back of upper legs), and the calves. Make sure you properly warm up before exercising—especially the hamstrings, as they are the most susceptible to injury.

When working out each muscle group, do multiple repetitions until fatigue, and in sets of two or three. You should also do at least two different exercises for each of these muscle groups. If using weights, increase these on each set of repetitions once they become easier. These exercises will improve the overall strength in your legs which will also improve your balance.

Best Exercises for Balance

Some leg exercises are even more effective and, if added to your leg workouts, can considerably improve your balance. The most superior type of leg exercise for balancing is static exercises, which extensively improve the strength of your muscles by giving you greater control for longer durations.

They also strengthen the smaller, supporting muscles, which otherwise might not have been trained during a routine workout.

Adding in one or two of these exercises to your leg workouts can help you greatly improve strength and control. Some examples of static exercises are wall-squat-holds, or squat-holds without wall support. These are common and amazingly effective moves. You can try to hold these positions for longer durations until you can reach one minute.

It's also simple to alter these exercises to make them more challenging. Over time, exercises just become easier, and to improve further you will need to make them more difficult. You can squat deeper, raise one leg, or add weight to your body—try holding dumbbell weights in each hand. Increasing the challenge of your exercises helps you to surpass plateaus and to improve your ability and performance.

Improving Core for Balance

Your core should also be targeted if you want to improve your balance. A strong core is important for stabilizing your whole body, allowing you to control many movements including balance. You can add multiple core and abdominal exercises two or more times weekly for a good result.

Core exercises don't typically take a great amount of time, generally lasting only ten to fifteen minutes for an effective workout. This can make them much easier to add into your week.

There are a copious number of exercises you can choose from to build your core. This makes it easy to swap them out for new ones when they become routine and less interesting. Core exercises can also be static, such as planks. Planks are great exercises to build strength in your abdominal muscles among others.

Some experts advise against sit-ups because of the risk that you can strain your neck, back, and spine. These exercises have the potential to cause injury, but they are very common, and many people continue to use them. As with any exercise, you don't want to feel any straining or sharp pain while performing them, only resistance and soreness as you try to break muscle fibers.

As mentioned, there's no shortage of different core exercises, so there are many safer ones you can choose from.

Improving Coordination for Balance

Coordination is another factor that determines your ability to balance. Your coordination is your ability to use different body parts together efficiently.

When a baseball player plays an outfield position, they simultaneously follow the ball in the air with their eyes, use their legs to run at the pace that will predictively catch up to the ball, jump while reaching an arm out to catch the ball in the air, then land back down on the ground.

This performance is aided by the player's ability to coordinate well.

There are many people with great coordination that may have it naturally or have developed it through their activities. Improving your coordination will not only improve your balance, but many other things that allow you more control over your body.

Playing sports is a great way to improve your coordination as it requires so many body movements. When you use multiple parts of your body synchronously, you develop your ability to coordinate well. Sports are great because there are so many different ones to choose from; you can easily find one that you like.

Balance & Core

At home, you could kick a soccer ball around the yard, throw a tennis ball against the wall, or play basketball. Just engaging in an activity that gets you moving around and using various parts of your body will be helpful to improving the neural connections in your cerebellum to develop your balance and posture.

Improving Balance with Mind-Body Workouts

Some workouts can develop your strength, balance, and coordination all at once. They can also greatly improve your mind.

Mind-body exercises such as Pilates and yoga are great examples of this. These build strength and coordination across the entire body, including the core and legs, and the stretches involved are very beneficial for your mind and body.

Another mind and body workout which includes more dynamic exercises is Tai Chi. This is a type of movement training in which you perform flowing movements from one posture to the next. You can build muscle strength and control and improve your coordination through these fluid and focused movements.

Tai Chi is intended to completely relax you, allowing you to connect your mind and body together as one. It can also help you release tense areas of your body to reduce stress.

Yoga, Pilates, and Tai chi are all great workouts you can do to improve your balance, even on your break days, as they can maximize your healing from the other workouts you've performed. As you learn more about these workouts, find one that's perfect for you and add it to your weekly routine.

Practice Balancing to Improve

Practicing balancing is important if you are trying to further your ability for more advanced activities. There are many things you can use for practice. The exercises and workouts mentioned before can support you as they improve muscle strength, control, and coordination.

Standing on one foot is something very basic you can start with—try to increase the duration you do this for over time to help your legs gain more control. You can do this almost any time, even at work.

Walking along a flat stable line on the ground will also improve your balance as you try to make it further and further without deviating.

It's important to know your abilities and to understand that many things you do come with risk—especially physical exercises. Proper footwear, equipment, and physical ability are necessary to avoid injury. When you perform exercises that require you to leave flat ground, your risk increases. That said, balancing bars that are properly manufactured are great for improving your balance even further, however they require a great amount of concentration and muscle control.

It's best to start with balancing bars that are closer to the ground, so there's less chance of injury if you fall. As your confidence and ability improve, you can raise these higher depending on what you want to accomplish. Many activities don't require such an advanced level of balancing, and strength and coordination training generally carry less risk.

Conclusion

Maintaining good balance is important for your health and ability to perform everyday activities. If you want to improve your balance, you

Balance & Core

can do so by building a strong and stable core and strengthening your legs. This can help you to develop great muscle control and a stable form.

You can improve even further with exercises and activities that require multiple body parts moving smoothly and accurately together. Sports and other physical activities are great practice for improving your coordination.

Balancing well is an essential part of fitness and can also support you in all your other fitness goals.

CHAPTER 11

Strength & Power

Increasing strength can be of top importance—this will give you better muscle definition and make you look more physically fit. But how can you be effective in your workouts to achieve this?

The single most important rule to increase strength is to increase weight. Weight that you lift, push, and pull.

What about power? What is power, regarding fitness?

Power is your speed of force—how quickly you can force weight in any direction. The speed that you can push, pull, and lift. Strength is the maximum amount of weight that can be performed; power is the speed that can be maximized during that performance. If you improve your strength and power, you can increase your ability to perform better.

Whether it is everyday activities, sports, or adventures, you can improve greatly for them. It doesn't matter if you're new to exercise or already very fit, you can improve to greater levels and enjoy your results. Depending on your goals, you may want to maximize the strength and size of your muscles, whereas others may want to focus on speed and power.

WELL-ROUNDED

You might just want to lose weight and build some strength to achieve good health, look great, and perform better. You can reach all these goals by adding strength and power training. Whether you have access to a gym or work out at home, there are many fantastic ways to increase your strength and power to achieve amazing results.

Maintaining Strength

To improve your strength, you will need a workout that consists of strength training exercises. If you're aiming to enhance the muscle size of your major muscle groups, they will need to be adequately and consistently trained.

Your nutrition and hydration needs may also need to be adjusted to support your workout.

It's also necessary to understand your restrictions and limitations to avoid injury and setbacks. There are many strength workouts you can find online or that you can obtain from your trainers. The example in the last chapter is an efficiency workout that can also work very well here.

This type of workout is basic and allows you to make the most of your time as you can quickly complete an effective workout.

- Day 1: Triceps and biceps.
- Day 2: Chest and back.
- Day 3: Legs and shoulders.
- Day 4: Endurance training.
- Day 5: Full body stretch or yoga.

As well as this, find two days during the week on either workout or non-workout days for core training. This is a common workout strategy

Strength & Power

to save time and get great results. When your body is properly warmed up and stretched, you can enter the workout phase.

Be sure to have access to water and take short breaks between exercises.

You will want to target each muscle group with one or two exercises twice a week, or complete three or four exercises once per week—this all depends on your schedule and time allowed for your workout.

Each exercise should contain at least two sets; three is better. Then cool down with stretches.

Completing these exercises each week will provide great results over a few months, even if you're new to fitness training. It will bring you to a certain level of fitness that you can then work to maintain alongside a proper diet. It may take longer than a few months if weight loss is your goal, but the results will come if you're consistent.

Exercising regularly will only maintain your current level with this approach. The following sections will discuss how to improve further and further.

It's important to understand that when beginning or returning to a workout plan, you should start by performing half of it and gradually build up to a full workout. There's no need to rush; people who have great fitness levels understand that it's achieved over time. It's better to wait for results rather than give yourself an injury that stops you from working out. Building up slowly can also reduce soreness so your muscles don't scream when you're walking around for the next few days. If you're new or returning to strength training, there will likely be some muscle soreness, so it's to be expected.

Results take time, starting slow will not delay them in any way.

WELL-ROUNDED

Changing Exercises to Improve Strength

Once you achieve a consistent workout pattern, and you have reached a certain level of fitness, you can maintain it using your current workout. You will have already improved your health and performance by going beyond the standard exercise requirements.

Strength training will provide great improvements to your mind and body, especially when combined with other workouts that include endurance and core training. If you wish to progress, there are many strategies that can be implemented into your current workout, or you can use more advanced methods to achieve even greater strength and muscle size.

Your body will grow accustomed to the workouts you perform, and you will no longer achieve greater performance once you hit a certain point—you will be only maintaining your current level of fitness. One way to improve your current workout is to change some of the exercises.

If you routinely perform bicep curls with dumbbells, try with a barbell.

You can also try different biceps exercises such as outward and twist curls instead of just inward curls.

Additionally, you can include hammer curls to exercise both the biceps and forearms, making both the upper and lower arms increase in size over time.

Different exercises and different variations of an exercise work the muscles in distinct ways that give them new challenges. This will recruit other smaller muscles in the arms, which can increase their overall size. This approach can be used for all muscle groups, you just need to change the exercises.

Strength & Power

Increasing Weight to Improve Strength

Changing your exercises often is great for keeping them interesting. Different workouts will help you stay engaged and enjoy them. It's a lot of work, but it's easier if you try new things.

When attempting to reach another level of fitness for strength and surpass a plateau, you will need to make the workout more challenging. You can do this by adding weight. Conveniently, you can increase your strength with your current workout by just adding weight. No need to learn very detailed and precise strength training programs, just add more weight.

You can add between one and five pounds and work with them until you reach your typical set of repetitions. If you normally perform ten or twelve repetitions in a set, and you use a fifteen-pound weight, you can advance to a twenty-pound weight. You can then use the twenty-pound weight until you reach ten to twelve repetitions again comfortably.

When this becomes easier and routine, add more weight.

You might get used to your normal routine and wonder why your fitness isn't improving when you're exercising every week. This is because your body is very adaptable and needs new challenges. Strength training is very straightforward.

As with all parts of the body, new challenges are what results in improvement.

If you want to grow bigger, there are also other exercises you can try and supplements you can take to give you the energy to lift heavier weight for longer and therefore break more muscle fibers during exercise.

These are fitness levels that many people aspire to reach and that certainly works for them.

However, attempting to reach these heights can compromise your health—fitness should you be about your mind and body and accomplishing new levels without forfeiting this. Supplementation should be considered with research and with your doctor's guidance to determine whether it's something that will both assist you with your fitness and maintain your health at the same time.

It's counterproductive if you develop health problems because of the choices you made to achieve great strength knowing the risk.

Your diet can also either improve your fitness or hold you back. Some people grow very big without the aid of supplements simply by eating the right diet. Finding a diet that supports muscle growth and then advancing your workout challenges will increase your strength to great levels.

Additional Ways to Improve Strength

Later, we will discuss how you can increase your power with speed of force. Performing the exercise with speed and increasing the weight over time will improve your power.

With strength training, you can perform exercises at a slow and even pace. This will help you to build better strength. You can also perform concentration exercises in which you focus on the target muscle group and squeeze the muscle as you lift, push, or pull.

This is a great way to engage as many muscle fibers as possible in the targeted muscle group to create multiple micro-tears. You want to feel some discomfort or soreness; if you feel nothing, it's likely you've only torn a few fibers, which will result in very little improvement. Sharp pains could be a sign you're exercising incorrectly, so this is not what you're looking for.

Strength & Power

You can also combine drop-sets, which include decreasing weight as you move through the next two sets of an exercise, or reverse-drop-sets, which include increasing the weight in the next two sets of an exercise.

It's important to note that this also involves decreasing the repetitions with heavier weights and increasing them with lighter weights. For example, for muscle growth, you improve using your heaviest weights that cause you complete fatigue at six repetitions, with your middle weights at about eight repetitions, and your lightest weights causing complete fatigue at ten to twelve repetitions.

Doing one exercise of reverse-drop-sets and then another for that same muscle group using drop-sets should effectively build muscle there. This can be done with exercises for the arms, legs, shoulders, and back and typically achieves great results if you increase the weight over time.

As an added method, try some super-sets where you do two separate exercises right after the other without a break, such as performing chin-ups and then going straight into curls. These are all effective methods to increase strength.

Strength Training Considerations

It's important to have a well-designed workout to increase strength, with the right diet and hydration that supports it. It helps to have the workout on a list where you can go from one exercise to the next, taking short breaks in between to recharge the energy.

You might go back and forth between opposing muscles to be more efficient. For example, doing one chest exercise, then one back exercise, and continuing to alternate throughout the workout. You should be monitoring yourself for dehydration and other side effects throughout the workout to avoid possible health problems and injury.

WELL-ROUNDED

If you're not looking to gain extensive muscle size, you can stay at weights you are comfortable with or increase your repetitions. This can result in great muscle definition and more endurance without creating a very bulky look.

If your workouts don't include the strength training you desire, or you're not achieving the results you want, you can ask a personal trainer for alternative regimens or purchase ones that are designed for the exact results you're looking for.

Improving Power

Improving your power can do amazing things for your fitness. It makes you faster and more capable. However, it can carry more risks during training. Increasing your power will include attempting exercises that are risky and that require very high intensity. There is risk for injury and your heart rate can get extremely high. You should determine with your physician whether these exercises are right for you and closely monitor yourself for side effects, your heart rate, breathing problems, dizziness, and dehydration.

It's very important to have an open, even, and clear workout area, as well as proper footwear, as some exercises require leaving the ground. Exercises may also require moving weights at a faster pace.

All these reasons increase the risk for injury, and you need to be comfortable with the risks you take.

If you choose to perform power exercises, and you are consistent with them, you can improve your fitness greatly. Adding power exercises to your workouts can give you explosive ability during sports and physical activities. With these, you aim to lift, push, or pull weights quickly with all your energy behind them.

Strength & Power

You shouldn't do this with any weights that go directly above the body.

For example, behind the back triceps extensions come very close to the spine and moving the weight quickly can cause contact with the head, spine, or shoulders. You cannot maintain or progress when you're injured. Performing power exercises designed for this type of training are much less risky and can provide you the results you're looking for.

There are effective and lower-risk exercises, such as pushups and pullups you can do either slowly for strength or fast for power. Later, this chapter will describe some ways to improve through adding to your body weight to create more resistance. Just as with strength exercises, you want to increase weight when the exercise becomes easy and no longer challenges you.

Power Exercises

There are some workouts that are entirely power focused, whereas others combine strength and power exercises to get the benefits of each. When performing both types, it's better to do power exercises first. If you use all your strength, you will lose some of your power, but if you do power exercises first, you can energize your muscles and perform better strength exercises.

For example, if you're performing squats with weights (holding a dumbbell in each hand, you can do the first three sets quickly, then do three sets of shoulder exercises, and then the next three sets of squats slowly. If you perform strength exercises first, your muscles will still be very fatigued.

This can be done without weights if you're a beginner, or you can do jump squats for your power exercise if you're more advanced.

There are many high intensity power workouts out there, plyometrics is one such example. This workout doesn't even require the use of weights, as it already incorporates enough challenge. During these exercises, your movements need to be as explosive as possible. Beginners will benefit from attempting a lower intensity and doing only half of the workout until you build your ability.

If you're more advanced and frequently perform power exercises, you may be able to complete up to an hour or more of plyometrics at high intensity. There are some other exercises and workouts that can also improve your power such as tire flipping, medicine ball throws, box jumps, burpees, boxing, and rowing.

If you like the idea of improving your power, look for workouts that include these or speak to your personal trainer for a mixture of strength and power exercises. You should also increase weight, jump higher, and lift faster. It's also important to have proper form and to avoid swinging your body.

Increasing Body Weight

Power and strength training can be done at home with the right equipment and methods, however it's better to have a workout partner for support as some of these exercises include risk for injury.

Home exercises that work great for this are pushups and pullups. You can even double the number of repetitions by tricking your body when you add more weight. Adding weight to your body can be complicated, but there are many ways you can do it safely to create more resistance and therefore more improvement.

Just as wrist and ankle weights are sometimes used in aerobics, you can add weight in other ways such as through a properly manufactured weight vest—which allow you to add weight over time. It's important to use all equipment as directed by the manufacturer, adequately fit and secure, and decide whether you are comfortable with the risks.

With weight vests, the weight should be evenly distributed so as not to carry too much in one area. If you note any signs of pain, you should not work through it—adjustments may be needed.

If you've plateaued at ten pullups for quite some time, and you want to overcome this, you can add weight to your body. Each week, or longer, add a few pounds of weight to the vest to increase your resistance. This will make your pullups and pushups more challenging. You can work with this weight until you reach ten pullups again, then add more weight and repeat.

Over the course of six months, you should have added between ten and twenty pounds or more. When you remove the weight vest and perform your pullups without that extra resistance, you should now be able to do up to twenty or more. This is how you increase your strength and power, by making a workout more challenging and building it up over time.

Just make sure you add weight safely, as some injuries, such as those to the back and neck, do not heal quickly. So, warmups, stretching, and correct use of weights, equipment, and workout space should all be used conscientiously. These techniques will produce amazing results if you keep challenging yourself, but it does not help to be injured for great lengths of time.

Conclusion

If you enjoy the level of fitness you've achieved and don't have the time or desire to advance, just performing the same exercises will maintain your current level just fine.

WELL-ROUNDED

After attaining any level of fitness, you'll notice you can perform everyday things much better. You are faster, stronger, and feel great. You are more competitive in sports and other physical activities. Results take time, sometimes many months to get to where you would like, but consistency and challenging yourself will help you get there.

Each person will have different goals: Some will want to look very muscular, some will want to improve at rock climbing, and others may just want to be in better shape. Fitness should be fun and enjoyable, and a way to improve yourself in any way you wish.

Sometimes there will be changes in your life, and you may go for long periods without exercise. If this happens, it's best to work your way back up slowly as you won't be at your previous fitness level. If it's only been a few months, it won't take long to get back to your previous level. There's no need to rush; your body can get back into shape quickly.

If you're just starting out, you will see a transformation in yourself over time. You can lose weight, carve out body fat, increase muscle size, and feel amazing. Power and strength are valuable parts of fitness that you can work at to improve.

CHAPTER 12

Endurance & Alternatives

You can achieve great strength and power from your training, but endurance is also a great part of fitness that you can improve. Endurance can be developed during strength training through lifting weights with more repetitions; for example, performing twenty repetitions in a set versus ten.

This is a great method for a more toned look as mentioned in the last chapter.

Yet, when you think about endurance training, you typically see them as long duration, aerobic activities that require extensive energy for your entire body to keep going. These activities involve having great levels of energy and stamina to perform. They require you to run, cycle, and swim repetitiously.

You can support your strength training with light endurance exercises, or you can focus more on endurance training and less on strength. It depends on your goals and what you would like to achieve. Endurance training can greatly improve your cardiovascular system, lungs, and how you utilize your energy.

This is very useful in sports and other physical activities, and can make great improvements to your health. Many people already have amazing endurance and compete in events such as marathons, ultra-distance cycling, and triathlons. These are incredible human achievements that take dedication and very hard work.

People that perform in these endurance competitions wake up each morning and run, cycle, or swim for numerous miles, building up incredible endurance capabilities.

It's not necessary to have a precise workout with targeted goals. Many people prefer this approach simply to follow their progress and reach objectives, but there are many ways to achieve a productive workout. Alternative workouts can be great for improving full-body fitness and may be much easier to add to your schedule each week.

There are also some great workouts that complement this training or work well on their own for you to improve your fitness. These are great for total body fitness, and are fun, relaxing, and can improve your mind and body.

Properly Preparing for Endurance Training

Endurance training has its risks, as many workouts do. Even more so because they can be high intensity and for long durations. All endurance exercises get your heart rate up very high and keep it there for extended periods of time. As always, you should speak to your physician to determine whether they are right for you.

You should also stay well hydrated, monitor your heart rate, wear proper gear, and consume an accommodating diet. Advanced endurance athletes typically perform their workouts between an extensive nine to twelve hours per week.

People that like to run marathons for fun may run for thirty minutes to over an hour, four to seven days per week.

Endurance & Alternatives

Most competitive runners will run for over an hour six or seven days per week to consistently improve their performance.

This is no easy task to accomplish. Those focusing on endurance build this over time, and just as with strength and power training, they must create more challenges when they plateau to reach another level of fitness. Endurance also requires great time commitment, however there are many that do make this commitment to build their endurance and subsequently achieve great things.

Not everyone needs to perform at this level of effort—there are many great things you can do with some improvement to your endurance. If you even exercised one-third of this amount you could still compete very well in sports and other physical activities. You may even just enjoy running or cycling for fun.

Thus, there's a range for how much you wish to train yourself. It really depends on what you'd like to accomplish.

Benefits of Endurance Training

As mentioned, there are many feats of endurance that can be accomplished through training for marathons and distance cycling. You can also use endurance training to help you in other sports. If you play basketball, soccer, or tennis, endurance training will help you to improve as it will increase your speed and give you more energy to keep going.

Endurance training is also extremely good for your cardiovascular system, lungs, and most other areas of your body. You can burn body fat when your glycogen reserves are depleted, so it can be a great workout strategy for weight loss.

It can also improve your metabolism and lower your risk for certain diseases. Furthermore, endurance training can reduce your resting heart rate—which is normally a sign of better health.

If you're not concerned with competitive endurance but want relatively good improvement, you can run, cycle, or swim for thirty minutes or more, four to seven days per week, and achieve great results. This will help you in sports, to run a marathon, or just be a fun way to improve your health. You can also choose one day per week to perform an aerobic exercise that complements your other workouts and saves time.

Those aiming to build very muscular bodies will typically only do very light aerobic exercises, often less than an hour and a half per week. It depends on your current workout plan and what you wish to achieve. However, you can get the benefits of both strength and endurance if you do a variety of workouts each week.

Advanced Endurance Training

To be competitive, or to achieve great endurance, you generally need to exercise for over an hour each day, and about six days per week. Many people that do this are very determined and it's what they really want. It's a lifestyle for them, and they will wake up every morning and run for ten to twenty miles without much discouragement.

Their bodies enter a different level because of how well they can use energy and they learn to endure great physical effort. They also retain a good diet to support their extensive exercise routines. Our bodies have an interesting way of giving you the energy you need, and then sustaining it for great periods of time.

There are three phases and systems to this process. The first, most immediate, system is called the phosphagen system. This does not require oxygen and is the initial burst of energy you get when you begin a run or lift a weight. This energy uses a small supply of creatine phosphate stored in the muscles and only lasts for a few seconds.

Endurance & Alternatives

The next is a short-term system called the glycolysis system, otherwise known as the anaerobic system, which also does not require oxygen. This can provide you with energy for up to about three minutes, but with slightly less power. This entire time, your heart and respiratory rate increases, glycogen, fats, or protein are broken down, and your blood carries oxygen and glucose to the cells for energy.

This leads you to the third system called the aerobic system. It's slower to act, and not as powerful, but will carry you for the long term. This explains how you get a burst of energy and start out very fast, but then reduce speed to a slower, more even pace.

These systems can also improve with proper nutrition, hydration, and training. Whatever your goals may be, there are so many options to improve your fitness.

Alternative Exercises

There are many alternative workouts that will also help you improve your strength and endurance training. There have been many focused training methods mentioned that have a specific goal in mind. You may want great strength, so your workout focuses on strength training: Lifting weights, core exercises, and some light cardio can accomplish this. You may work on a couple of body parts each day to build them up. Another person may choose to run for ten miles every day to build endurance for a marathon.

If you have a focused plan in mind such as these, it's great for getting you to your goals. However, if your goal is weight loss, overall fitness, or just total body health there are many full-body workouts that you can perform a few days per week that can give you amazing health and fitness without a very detailed plan.

Just performing these workouts and trying to get through them to the end will make great improvements to your mind and body. They are also interesting and fun to do each day, which will help you stay engaged.

These workouts are also just as adaptable, so exercises can be removed and replaced with others to make them interesting and more challenging. Many of these workouts will require building endurance, strength, and skill over time to perform each exercise correctly and to complete the entire workout.

This should not discourage you—each time you return to the workout you will get better.

They can also include high-intensity exercises as well as static holds and difficult positions, so you will need to understand your risks and progress your ability over time. If you stay consistent with your full-body workouts, you will soon see great improvements to your body.

High-Intensity Interval Training (HIIT)

An amazing, high intensity full-body workout that's great for weight loss and building incredible fitness is high-intensity interval training (HIIT). This workout includes many different exercises, both resistance and aerobic, in which the goal is to move from one exercise to the next at different intensities, or with short breaks.

It's also possible to use this for strictly strength and endurance training, but this example will describe how you achieve a fun, full-body workout to improve your overall fitness. There are many HIIT workouts you can purchase or get from your trainer that contain a list of exercises to work with.

Some require very minimal equipment to perform the exercises as well.

Endurance & Alternatives

Always ensure you have water, proper workout gear, a clear area, and warmup, stretch, and monitor your body for side effects such as breathing problems or dizziness. One option is to perform an exercise at high-intensity, and then the next at low-intensity, and alternate in this way throughout the workout.

Alternatively, you can perform one exercise at high-intensity, take a short break, and the next exercise at high-intensity again. These can be fun exercises, such as pushups, pullups, running in place, box jumps, or squats. You just move from one to the next giving each your best effort.

It's very helpful to have your workout area prepared beforehand and basically have stations where you can move from one workout to the next without needing to prepare as you go. Another great advantage of this type of workout is that you can make it as long or short as you like.

If the workout comes out at an hour of exercise, you can choose to only perform half because of limited time and do the other half the following day. This removes a barrier to exercise, just as mentioned in chapter eight. On days you have more time, you can try the full workout.

Mind-Body Workouts and Sports

Other alternative workouts such as yoga, Pilates, and Tai Chi were mentioned previously. These workouts can help with strength, flexibility, and relaxation. Performing them as your main workout or adding them to your week can help you round out your fitness. As mentioned before, they can help you heal from your other workouts, too.

These workouts also have many challenging positions—to perform them accurately you may need to increase your strength and flexibility. They are also changeable, so when they become routine, there are many different moves and styles that you can choose from.

WELL-ROUNDED

Sports has been mentioned many times; this also counts as a workout. You can sign-up for different interesting sports, and they can greatly improve your speed, strength, and endurance. It's important to find physical activity you enjoy doing so you stay interested and engaged in your fitness. Even a low intensity run or walk in the park will help you improve your energy to do more.

Cycling and swimming are also fun physical activities you can enjoy and improve your fitness with. Swimming can help you to build strength and endurance and works well for people with certain restrictions who are unable to perform other exercises.

Finding ways to work around your obstacles will allow you to be more active, improve your fitness, and feel great.

Advanced Workouts

If you really want to take your fitness to an extreme level, and you're already very experienced and want something more challenging, you may want to try something that combines HIIT and yoga together.

Calisthenics is a gymnastic type of workout where people build their strength and endurance to achieve very difficult positions and holds. This requires some of the most risk involved in exercising, but there are many ways to do this safely and achieve great things over time. As with all exercise, you want to be sure you know the risks and make a careful decision about safely engaging in it.

Calisthenics includes exercises that are normally either endurance strength, or strength holds. This means getting into difficult balanced positions and holding them. Other workouts can be performed to accommodate this workout, or some will choose to perform only calisthenics. The holds and endurance training focus on total body strength, but some will primarily target upper body strength and core.

There are various holds, such as triceps holds, squats, hanging from a pullup bar, L-sits, and human flag. Many of the exercises target the shoulders and core to build strength and balance for handstands, handstand pushups, fist-stand pushups, and others. Calisthenics is certainly not for everyone, it requires time and effort to make progress and it carries more risk.

This just describes how extreme fitness can be and some more interesting ways that people can try to improve.

Conclusion

Endurance exercise is a great approach to improving fitness and has many health benefits. You can choose to add it into your week just to improve your fitness, or it can be an entire lifestyle where you're passionate about it and want to see how far you can perform.

If you make exercise fun and start seeing improvement, you are likely to keep it up. This helps you keep fitness in your life, so you can become healthier, stronger, and look and feel great. There is no need to rush—being consistent and enjoying yourself will keep you engaged and ensure you continually improve.

LIVE WELL

One would only need to walk through a forest to see an abundance of living things enduring the elements of their environment to survive, all managing to live and flourish in their own distinct and wonderful ways. You hear their sounds of joy, see their beauty, and smell their intriguing scents.

You too are a living, thriving, and unique being with remarkable abilities you use to traverse through life. You have incredible potential, and your differences set you apart from everything in the world and allow you to paint something different in existence.

A belief system is something entirely distinctive to each person, and it develops as they interpret the world around them. There will be people that believe happiness is the goal in life; others may believe that it is survival and reproducing for life to continue.

Many believe that it's our connection with God.

Some think that we're in a video game designed by something greater.

If you're here experiencing, then existence has potential to be infinite—there is so much more to discover. You are a teardrop that has landed into this space and time, and because you're water, you can flow in any direction.

WELL-ROUNDED

When you encounter a barrier, you adapt and flow past it. When you meet other teardrops flowing, you merge with them to become stronger and more powerful to pass even greater barriers.

This book has conveyed many ideas and strategies you can use to improve yourself so you can thrive and pass barriers. Combine these with your experiences and knowledge to further develop yourself and design new ways to pursue your interests and connect with others.

Every new experience you have will allow you to improve your knowledge and ability. Therefore, you're limited by your experiences, and knowing this makes you limited by your *will* to experience.

Just as the elements and finding food create challenges for wildlife, we too will have many difficulties, and many barriers in the way of our ability to thrive and live exceptionally. However, you can develop your mind and body to endure and enjoy the world around you and to engage in it with your unique abilities.

You can overcome your barriers to live well.

Live Well, The End.

ABOUT THE AUTHOR

Located in Oregon, Alexander lives with his teenage son. They love the outdoors and exploring new surroundings. The author is passionate about knowledge, health, and fitness. His college studies are in biology and psychology. He has also studied economics and statistics and has over twenty years of investment and money management experience. Alexander is certified as a Personal Trainer and Lifestyle Wellness Coach and is determined to help clients and others accomplish more and live well.

If you enjoyed this book and the information within, please take a few moments to write a review wherever you may have purchased it. Thank you.

For more health and fitness content, feel free to visit our blog: www.well-rounded.org/blog-posts

Made in the USA
Coppell, TX
02 January 2024

27159313R00134